STOP BEING SO NICE

How to Set Boundaries,
Overcome People-Pleasing, and Live Authentically

By
Juan David Arbeláez

Published by
MENTE | LATERAL

STOP BEING SO NICE
Juan David Arbeláez

All rights reserved. No part of this book may be reproduced or transmitted in any form or by any electronic or mechanical means, including photocopying, recording, or any information storage and retrieval system, without written permission from the author.

COPYRIGHT©2024 Juan David Arbeláez

20241108

Index

Introduction 1

Say Goodbye to Toxic Kindness 2

The High Price of People-Pleasing 8

How to Stop Being a Doormat 13

Boundaries and Responsibilities 17

Rewrite Your Rules 21

Guilt: Wise Counselor or Ruthless Witch? 24

Breaking Free from Guilt 26

The "Apologitis" Epidemic 28

The Power of Silence 32

The Art of Saying "NO" and Being Selectively Available 35

Let Go, Release, and Flow 38

Shedding Your Skin and the Myth of Static Identity 42

The Art of Not Taking Anything Personally 46

The Fear of Rejection 51

Stop Carrying Other People's Problems 56

Authentic Relationships 58

Healthy Selfishness 62

Authenticity: The Secret to Fulfilling Sexuality 66

Social Media 69

At Work 73

The "I Don't Know Yet" Technique 77

Alcohol and Drugs: The False Social Lubricant 79

Energy Vampires 82

"Mockying": Bullying in Adulthood 85

The World's Worst Neighbor 88
How to Deal with Hypocrites 92
The Moochers' Bazaar 97
Asking Without Shame 102
Nothing Is As Important As It Seems 106
Don't Take Anything at Face Value 109
Epilogue: A Postscript to the Golden Rule 113
Appendix 1: A Course in Sarcasms 117
Appendix 2: 19 Missions to Stop Being Too Nice 139
Appendix 3:
The 10 Commandments of Truly Authentic People 146
Appendix 4: Mephistophelian Contract 150
About the Author 152

Introduction

No one ever said a book needs to have an introduction—so let's not dwell here too long, as we have plenty to explore. That said, I'd like to highlight two important things before we dive in:

First, I recommend reading just one or two chapters per day to fully absorb the content. Take your time—there's no rush.

Second, as a native Spanish speaker and self-published author, this book has been translated from Spanish to English using a combination of tools and personal effort. As a result, you might come across the occasional minor error. I trust, however, that the message will come through loud and clear despite these imperfections.

Now, let's get started.

Juan David Arbeláez

Say Goodbye to Toxic Kindness

Is life really simple, or is it rather a mess of challenges, entanglements, and contradictions? This question has been philosophers' daily bread for centuries, forcing each generation to rethink what we believe we know about existence.

But let's be honest, saying life is simple can sound like a children's tale. Leaving behind the carefree days of youth brings responsibilities and complications that pile up like dirty dishes in a sink. Conflicts, frustration, and inequality become more real, making simplicity seem like an unattainable chimera.

However, I believe these complications reflect our inner world more than reality itself. Epictetus[1], the Stoic philosopher, said it well: "We are not disturbed by things or situations, but by our judgment about them." So, are we living in a shared objective reality, or is each of us trapped in our own world, giving unique meaning to what we each experience? Spoiler alert: in this world... everyone... lives in their own world!

Breaking free from the bonds of what we believe to be life's norm isn't easy. We all have an internal

---

[1] Greek philosopher (50-135 CE) who began life as a slave. His teachings focused on personal freedom, self-discipline and accepting what's beyond our control. His main work 'The Enchiridion' remains influential in modern psychology and self-help literature.

critical voice that never quiets, a voice that reproaches us for setting boundaries, punishes us for any moment of honesty, and makes us feel guilty for saying "NO" to someone or like idiots for not standing our ground. We doubt ourselves, fear "what others will say," imagine we'll awaken others' anger if we speak up or that by being honest, we'll push them away.

But... perhaps life isn't as overwhelming as we think. Maybe it's the lens through which we look that distorts reality. What would happen if we removed that filter and saw things as they really are? Would we be temporarily blinded by such clarity? Could we embrace that light with courage?

The real challenge isn't in pretending life is easy, but in examining how our perspective affects it. Change doesn't happen by waiting for everything to simplify; change occurs when we adjust our way of seeing things. And this is something only each individual can do for and by themselves.

Yes, people really can transform their mindset, and anyone, regardless of their circumstances, can find clarity and peace. I know it sounds ambitious, and doubt is natural, but that doesn't mean it isn't true. However, achieving that change requires commitment to honest and often uncomfortable self-evaluation. Just because something is difficult doesn't mean it's impossible. If there's a will to make an effort, who knows? Instead of feeling trapped in a cycle of confusion and frustration, we might find an open path full of potential.

So let's begin by accepting a painful truth: fear moves people more than the desire to achieve virtue. That's how things are, and that's what we're going to address and change. At least, within ourselves.

Kindness has always been seen as something positive. It's associated with caring for others, doing good, avoiding confrontation, and pleasing everyone. But sometimes, being too nice is actually a disguise for fear of disapproval, not a genuine virtue, and therefore, this habit can lead to hidden resentments and exhaustion while we drift away from who we really are.

Here's a provocative question: Have you noticed that those who seem to achieve everything aren't always the kindest people? Look at kings, politicians, artists, athletes, and you'll see that kindness often appears to be just a facade in certain contexts. I say it's a provocative question, not against them, but against ourselves. They know something many of us resist accepting: that being excessively nice can halt our progress.

You can't please everyone. Research confirms it. Excessive people-pleasing has tangible disadvantages: worse credit ratings, more debt, and greater financial risk. Meanwhile, those who truly prioritize themselves tend to face fewer problems and reap more successes.

Even in relationships, being too nice can backfire. Predictability can bore others who seek a challenge. And although the effects vary between men and women, excessive kindness isn't always rewarded, nor is it attractive.

If overwhelm and guilt are constant, perhaps our excessive niceness is to blame. It might be preventing us from being truly honest about what we really want, resulting in a mask that convinces no one and brings more disadvantages than advantages.

Breaking free from this trap won't be a quick process; it's like escaping from a straitjacket made of beliefs that wrongly associate assertiveness with selfishness. But I'll say it again: just because something is difficult doesn't mean it's impossible.

How do we break free from this straitjacket? To begin with, we must recognize that your personality isn't set in stone. With practice and a different attitude, you can be both assertive and kind, without falling into the trap of being either a bulldozer—who runs over everyone to get ahead—or a doormat—a rag everyone uses to clean dirt, fix things, and then discard in a corner when they're done and it's dirty.

The key lies in focusing on your own needs without ignoring others', but understanding that everyone must go at their own pace and learn their own lessons. Repeat this until it's engraved in your brain: it's time to finally include yourself in your list of priorities and, moreover, to list yourself first.

It's crucial to understand that prioritizing yourself isn't a selfish act, but a necessity to be well and thus offer your best to others. Prioritizing your well-being doesn't mean trampling others or acting inconsiderately; it's about finding a balance where you recognize that your own well-being is the foundation for supporting and caring for those around you. Though you're not the center of the universe, you are the center of your own world and the fundamental pillar for those who depend on you—like your children if you're a parent and they're still young. How could you ensure others' well-being if you neglect your own? Remember that you can't give what you don't have, so taking care of yourself is the first step to caring for others effectively and sustainably.

In the journey I propose in these pages, we must be ready to question some deeply rooted beliefs. We're going to find what filters distort our worldview and seek to CHANGE them.

This won't happen by magic, and just reading this book won't do it all for you—I repeat that achieving that change is your responsibility alone. But here's my guarantee: any change you embrace after reading these pages will be a gain. A step toward a more authentic life. Every small shift in perspective can reveal the simple and refreshing essence of life that, in reality, has always been waiting to be appreciated and that, to answer the initial question, isn't as difficult as everyone believes it to be. Your vision of the world is what matters to you. And that's what we're going to improve.

The High Price of People-Pleasing

We all love to be liked and accepted. It's part of the human experience. But constantly trying to please everyone has its dark side. The endless effort to gain others' approval drains you, leaving you with superficial relationships and an inner void that no pleasure seems able to fill. Being excessively nice holds back your progress, opens the door to manipulation, and ties your hands, both personally and professionally.

This story repeats itself everywhere: the employee who, starting a new job, believes that to advance they must stay silent, swallow their pride, and shoulder everyone else's responsibilities; the girlfriend who gave up everything for her partner; the friend who always lends money to those in trouble; the person who endures bullying - or "burling," as I prefer to call it - from their "friends" because they have no one else.

Being the nice one in the group can be a one-way ticket to frustration. Putting others' approval on a pedestal means neglecting what truly matters. Fear of rejection controls your steps until your ideals crumble or, at least, come to a grinding halt.

But let's clarify something: we shouldn't confuse genuine kindness with the desperate need to please and be approved. The first comes from empathy and good manners; the second, from insecurity and fear of rejection. People-pleasers spend their lives trying to be liked, as if that would guarantee love and acceptance.

This fear usually has its roots in childhood, when our self-esteem becomes trapped in the expectations of authority figures around us. If a child learns they're only valued when they please others, they'll carry that burden into adulthood, letting others determine their worth.

Codependency also plays its part. That's how love ends up seeming like something that must be earned by meeting expectations and avoiding conflicts. In these cases, people-pleasers push aside their own needs to feed their partners', creating a toxic and unbalanced dynamic.

On the other hand, here's another hard truth to accept: people-pleasing isn't as selfless as it appears. In many cases, this compliance is an attempt to control how others see us. It's a favor expecting another in return. Those who always say yes and do anything for anyone are actually trying to manage others' opinions. But in the end, this controlling impulse distorts their self-perception and tangles their relationships in lies.

In psychology, there's something called the "spotlight effect" that describes how people overestimate how much others notice their actions and appearance. This effect makes us believe we're always under an imaginary spotlight, like in a theater performance, being observed and judged. But the reality is that most people are too busy with their own lives to notice every detail of our behavior or appearance.

This "spotlight effect"[2] reinforces the need to please everyone, convincing those who suffer from it that they live under constant scrutiny from others.

A problem with this false spotlight effect is that many take advantage of it: your excessive kindness under this effect becomes a manipulation mechanism used by others. The price of being an eternal people-pleaser is high. Living while postponing your needs and suppressing your feelings to prioritize others brings stress, resentment, and eventually, depression. These people take on too much, becoming easy prey for those who recognize their condition.

To break this cycle, you need to question what drives it. Your self-esteem shouldn't depend on what others think. Building a solid foundation of self-acceptance and learning to say "NO" is vital.

The root of your need to please everyone lies in beliefs formed before you even knew what self-esteem

---

[2] In psychology, there's something called the 'spotlight effect'" Footnote: "Psychological phenomenon first described by Thomas Gilovich (1998). Studies show people overestimate by 2-3x how much others notice their appearance/actions. A Cornell study found only 50% of observers noticed obvious changes subjects thought everyone would spot.

was. Comparing yourself to siblings, school friends, colleagues, or your environment made you think your worth depended on how useful or likable you were. It's as if you believed you were a lamp that only shines when others turn it on, instead of having your own light.

Fear of confrontation also works against you: anxiety about avoiding making others uncomfortable, shame, or fear of emotional destabilization push you to stay quiet instead of speaking up or setting clear boundaries.

Moreover, mixing the desire to please with the idea of being "good" takes this to another level. From childhood, we're taught that being nice is great, but indirectly we're led to believe that being honest and thinking of ourselves is almost a flaw, that it's selfish. How many ridiculous demands have we yielded to more out of fear or not wanting to appear selfish than for any real reason?

To stop pleasing at all costs, you need to identify the rules governing your life and separate what truly resonates with you from what's just inherited baggage from the past. A common trap is assuming too much responsibility for others' emotions. After all, you can't control how others feel - disappointment and anger are part of the game, and accepting that others are free to feel them takes a weight off your shoulders.

Even misinterpreted religion can reinforce toxic perfectionism, making you measure every thought against unattainable divine standards. Letting go of that paralyzing guilt that someone in the clouds hears, sees, and judges everything you do in your passing through Earth opens the door to true faith, self-compassion, and deeper connections.

So, what are you going to do? Keep carrying the heavy backpack of excessive niceness or dare to walk toward your most authentic and fulfilled version? For those brave enough to try, the whole world opens up. Yes, it's difficult, but the rewards are real and lasting. It's time to stop being a doormat, stop being everyone's scapegoat, and start living for yourself!

How to Stop Being a Doormat

We're all chasing some fantasy of greatness, and in doing so, we've come to believe that pleasing others is somehow part of the recipe for achieving it. At the end of the day, we end up exhausted, wondering when the hell life turned into an endless race where we make no progress. We're sold the idea that being kind and selfless is the master key to successful relationships, but nobody tells you that this path often leads to stagnation, resentment, and burying your own dreams in a swamp of compliance.

Putting yourself first isn't selfish—it's common sense: it's survival. How many times have you heard on an airplane that in case of decompression, you should put your oxygen mask on before helping others? Well, that rule applies to life too. Saying "NO" to what doesn't align with your priorities is self-care, not coldness. Doing so isn't weakness either—it's marking your territory. Being clear about what you need and knowing when to say no opens the door to more authentic experiences.

This is where the importance of boundaries comes in. Having clear boundaries is what truly gives us control and power. The ability to say "NO" and prioritize our needs over others' demands gives us an invaluable sense of freedom. Without these boundaries, we float in a sea of others' expectations, believing that being nice all the time is a virtue, without realizing that behind that kindness lies only stress and frustration accumulated from the thousand-and-one times others have walked all over us. And that ends up taking its toll on the body: aches, digestive problems, the classic signs that something's wrong even when we pretend to be calm. Yes, the body manifests everything: that time you went to the doctor and they said what you had "was stress," was simply their way of telling you that you need to change something in your mental model, because your physical body disagrees.

Not establishing boundaries robs you of clarity about who you really are. Prioritizing others' feelings over your own puts you in a cycle of anxiety and guilt that destroys any genuine relationship. Understanding and acting on these boundaries transforms relationships from a game of endurance to one of respect and authenticity. Yes, that time your friends or family saw you broken down crying, and in their attempt to console you said "why haven't you said/done/spoken about this, etc.?" they were also demanding that you set boundaries at a moment when you needed them.

You have to know what you really want. You have to define who you really are, not how you expect others to see you. You have to be brutal with yourself and stop giving value to what doesn't deserve it, or to what promises value but doesn't deliver. Regularly connecting with what you truly want can change your whole way of making decisions. That's defining boundaries. That's establishing your principles. That's telling the world: "This is who I am. This is how I am, and this is how I want to be." This introspection, from everyday things to major changes, gives us clarity. These are your principles, and they're non-negotiable.

If you can't define who you are, then try approaching it from the other side: a good starting point is knowing what you DON'T want. From there, exploring alternatives becomes easier. Constantly asking yourself "What do I want?" and "What do I NOT want?" helps reconnect with your authentic SELF and makes decisions easier.

The thing is, people tend to know what they want, but often feel forced to swallow their desires to fit others' expectations. Over time, this creates limiting beliefs and the feeling that wanting something is selfish. But desires aren't good or bad—they just are. Ignoring them doesn't make anyone more virtuous; it only worsens frustration and strains relationships.

On the other hand, not knowing what you want is more common than it seems, especially after years of living to please others. A "I don't know" in response to the question "What do you really want?" might be hiding a fear of facing what you truly feel. It might be a sign of preferring the familiar and comfortable, even if unsatisfying, rather than embarking on the journey of self-discovery.

The way to face this is with curiosity. Always think that everything brings something valuable with it: When faced with anything unexpected—good or bad—always think: "I wonder what I'll discover? What can I get from this? What does this have for me?" This can turn any experience into something positive.

If you don't set boundaries, you let others take control over your opinions and decisions. This leads to believing that being "open-minded" means others' opinions matter more and that you're just a vehicle for their desires. Breaking free from that trap means giving full space to your own perspective, regardless of whether you're facing an expert or a novice who might contradict or not understand you. The confidence to express what you think starts from within. Seeking constant external validation causes confusion and limits your ability to change what you want to improve.

Boundaries and Responsibilities

I know it's cliché, but let's use the well-known garden fence metaphor. This fence constitutes a physical boundary where one property ends and another begins. One side is the garden for plants and play, and the other side is for something else or belongs to someone else. The same happens with you as a person when you establish clear boundaries: you know exactly where your rights and responsibilities begin and where others' start. Without this clarity, everything blends together, becomes a sticky mess, and you end up carrying everyone else's problems.

This lack of clear boundaries is a recipe for disaster: you create connections full of misunderstandings where everyone thinks they're the star of the show but no one knows the steps to the dance. Anyone can step on you or walk all over you. Every attempt to resolve a discussion or minor issue transforms into a trial, where one person brings up the topic and the other becomes defensive, derailing the conversation and magnifying the problem with phrases like: "How dare you say that?" Thus, any real problem hides better than a cat in a storm, especially if the person raising it is one of those who always wants to be the neighborhood's good guy. Instead of resolving the conflict, we focus on calming negative emotions without addressing the root of the matter.

In the long run, the result is a predictable disaster: unresolved problems pile up and limited communication becomes an insurmountable wall to real understanding. The key to healthy relationships lies in setting those boundaries and knowing who does what. With these foundations, interactions become more authentic and lighter, without carrying responsibilities that aren't yours.

The point is to redefine responsibility: you can have empathy without throwing your own boundaries overboard. Nowadays, thanks to epidemics like the WOKE mental virus, where slogans like "don't let privilege cloud your empathy" are thrown around left and right, setting boundaries or having privileges seems to be a crime - but it's not! It's just a trap that depersonalizes your responsibilities and rights: a distortion that life is all about rights and no duties. That's why, now more than ever, rethinking what responsibility means might seem crazy. But, although it might sound like a fairy tale to newer generations, everyone is responsible for their own emotions.

Internalizing the idea that "we're not responsible for how others feel" is like taking a breath of fresh air and facing a challenge at the same time. It might seem like you're ignoring others' emotions, but that's not the case. We're so used to protecting others' feelings at the cost of our own that the current world follows this trend, creating increasingly fragile and malleable people - or as I prefer to call them: softies.

This obsession with not hurting anyone holds us back. Many think: "If I say what I think, I'll surely offend them." This idea turns any honesty into a minefield, blocking any form of real connection. Seeing others as incapable of handling discomfort prevents building authentic bonds, creating the false image that everyone must be handled with kid gloves. That's precisely why we talk about newer generations as being "snowflakes."

Let everyone handle their own emotions. We're all capable of doing it. And if you can't do it now, you'll surely manage later. Time heals everything, and if it can't heal it, well, it dissolves it. This way, you release the weight of wanting to control others' reactions and make room for mutual respect.

Letting go of that nonsense about being responsible for everything others feel around us, and understanding that this was never a task assigned to us at birth can only be liberating. Finding the balance between empathy and maintaining solid boundaries is essential to thrive, both personally and professionally.

Setting boundaries isn't selfish; it's an act of self-love that creates an environment where relationships can flourish in a balanced and genuine way. It helps build a space conducive to authentic and healthy connections. By marking and maintaining these boundaries, you generate a dynamic that respects both your needs and preferences as well as those of others. Boundaries aren't walls, but guides for respectful and fruitful relationships. They allow you to interact with clarity and confidence, ensuring mutual understanding and respect.

Declare with conviction and without fear of what they might say, "This is where I stop! From here on, it's up to you."

Period.

Rewrite Your Rules

The truth is, when we arrive at this game called life, nobody gives us an instruction manual, so each of us must distill our own principles and values to create our rules. But how do we decide which rules to follow and, more importantly, how do we create our own rules?

Sure, there are basic rules, those societal laws that most people accept without blinking and that help maintain - partly - social balance. But daily decisions are governed by an internal algorithm that dictates how you speak, act, and relate to others. After years of trying to please everyone, your authenticity vanishes, and you end up making decisions based on others' expectations. This tangle of rules silently installs itself in your rational and subconscious mind. Each external criticism infiltrates your mental list of things you "shouldn't" question, even without you noticing. Thus, the most ridiculous rules can resurface in absurd social situations:

- You should do this.

- You should go out more.

- You should change that face.

Should... Should... SHOULD! The result is a limited catalog of permitted behaviors, governed by self-censorship and externally imposed "shoulds." Following these rules drains you and turns life into a cage fearful of others' judgment. Reviewing that list of "shoulds" can be revealing. Do they still make sense? Or are they obsolete limits you once imposed on yourself that now only hold you back?

Many of us carry rules we never asked for, norms to avoid raising our voice, contradicting others, or always being loyal to what we want. Realizing these chains can be broken is vital. So do yourself a favor, explore your inner self and answer right now: What are three of those "shoulds" you often repeat and what guilt do they carry? The most tyrannical rules cling to values engraved in the soul. Letting go of them isn't easy, but if you reflect, you'll discover that this constant struggle to be worthy of love and acceptance is more a cry for childish validation than a real connection: Living to be enough is a pathetic trap.

The next step is to change those old rules for ones that really matter. Transform your "shoulds" into "coulds." Adjust your list. These rules must be yours, built to sustain a life that resonates with you.

Start with your internal "shoulds." Using "could" instead of "should" in your inner dialogue opens a world of possibilities:

- "I should lose weight" / "I could lose weight"

- "I should change jobs" / "I could change jobs"

- "I should tell my parents" / "I could tell my parents"

The difference is that "should" makes you feel guilty and "could" doesn't. The first is an internal whip and the second is a light that helps you think better about how to do things.

Likewise, when someone throws a "should" at you, respond fearlessly by saying "or I could!" This is setting boundaries; no one has the right to tell you what you "should" do, and you're reclaiming your power of decision and making it clear.

The "coulds" give you options to choose better and not carry guilt. At the end of the day, more than any external obstacle, it remains solely your matter of doing or not doing what you COULD do: don't let it become an excuse to postpone what you know deep down you COULD take advantage of. There's a long way from saying to doing, but in between... IT'S ALWAYS YOUR OWN CHEST!

"You could really do what you said you could do!"

Guilt: Wise Counselor or Ruthless Witch?

The old internal rules we mentioned are like ghosts that frighten you with imaginary visions of rejection or guilt if you dare to break them. But let's be clear, these fears are pure theater. When you follow your inner compass, truths you didn't want to see start coming to light. Saying "NO" or setting boundaries hasn't triggered the end of the world yet. In fact, living life your way can bring quite pleasant surprises.

Of course, changing the script isn't a walk in the park. Guilt appears when you redraw your boundaries, this is when guilt tends to assume its role as a ruthless witch. But there are two types of guilt: the one that's actually useful and the one that's holding you back. The first reminds you that you're straying from your principles, it's like your internal GPS keeping you from losing sight of who you really want to be. That's the one telling you to get back on track in a different way - that's the wise counselor. The second is pure toxic waste, corrosive, based on the idea that you deserve to suffer for your mistakes. That's, as we pointed out, the ruthless witch that curses and manipulates you at will.

Instead of torturing yourself, connect with what lies beneath: the pain, disappointment, fear of being alone. Responding to these emotions with empathy opens the door to real change. They're uncomfortable emotions, but that's all they are: they can be overcome, and with each passing minute, doing so becomes easier.

Real change isn't a willpower competition; it's a pact with yourself. Slowing down the revolutions, feeling your body, listening to what guilt has to say, leads you to clarity. That's where you distinguish what really matters and how you want to position yourself in this world. Creating habits aligned with that vision is a recipe for lasting changes.

Absurd guilt is born from rigid rules that overlooked your values. These rules drag you into a cycle of constant self-criticism, selling you the illusion that only your own perfection or others' approval redeems you. Letting go of the obsession with perfection is essential. Believing that peace and happiness will come after the next achievement is a scam. Even the biggest successes only bring a brief respite before the next challenge. Understanding this is the first step to stop running in circles.

Use guilt to learn and adjust, never to flagellate yourself.

Breaking Free from Guilt

Well, no one is, nor should be, the manager of others' emotions or demands. There's no need to say "YES" to everything. Everyone must figure out how to satisfy their own needs.

Guilt visits us all from time to time, but staying stuck in a loop wondering "Why me? Why didn't I do this?" is the fastest way to ruin your mental and emotional health. If there's something you need to convince yourself of, it's this: guilt, without proper use, is as useful as a fork in soup. Drowning in it until it nullifies you is like torturing yourself without achieving anything.

The trick is to recycle that guilt into something useful. If a situation leaves you with a bitter feeling, acknowledge that something went wrong and that's it. No drama, just the first step to ensure you don't mess up the same way next time.

To see if something really aligns with your self-interest, always ask yourself the following:

1. What do I really want?

2. How much do I want it?

3. What needs am I meeting?

4. What effect will this have on others?

5. How can they meet their own needs?

6. If I don't do something for others, will anything serious happen to them?

If the desire exists and the collateral damage is minimal, go ahead, zero guilt. Repressing it only builds frustration and resentment, while allowing it instills energy, confidence, and even generosity.

When you feel you've really messed up, identify where your guilt comes from and take a moment to imagine how you would have liked to act. It's like mental rehearsal, so next time you'll have things clearer. Call it adjusting your "life algorithm" if you want, but learning and improving your reaction, even in a mental scenario, isn't optional - it's indispensable.

From this point, the commitment is to yourself. Drop the empty words and make sure to remember the lesson next time. This internal pact turns guilt into a spark for improvement, not an anchor that drags you down.

Stopping feeling guilty isn't the same as wiping the slate clean while ignoring your mistakes. It's telling yourself, "Okay, I messed up, what can I take from this to avoid or improve it in the future?", learning from the situation, and having the courage to try not to repeat the same scene. That's knowing yourself, moving forward, and evolving. Everything else is a waste of time.

The "Apologitis" Epidemic

Many people go through life following rules that don't even exist, terrified of crossing imaginary lines and habitually apologizing even for breathing. In Latin America, and even more so in my country, Colombia, the word "sorry" and its variants like "excuse me," "my bad," etc., infiltrate conversations like a nervous tic, filling uncomfortable silences or softening phrases that need no soothing. I like to call this condition "Apologitis." It's the compulsion to apologize for everything without reason, a verbal crutch that's used even when you haven't done anything worthy of reproach.

Apologizing meaninglessly is like not apologizing at all: the word loses all its impact. Someone who makes excuses for everything without justification sends a clear message: This person doesn't know where they stand and doesn't respect themselves. And if someone doesn't respect themselves, why should others? This habit turns those who suffer from it into people who retreat at the slightest shadow of confrontation.

- "Sorry, oh my gosh, could I...?"

- "I'm sorry, I don't mean to bother, but..."

- "I apologize, may I ask you a question?"

These and many other seemingly harmless phrases are blank shots that Apologitis sufferers fire without thinking, reflecting deep insecurity and an irrational fear of rejection. Nobody needs to apologize for existing.

The point is that real apologies should be reserved for what truly deserves them: when you've made a genuine mistake or caused real harm. Apologizing out of fear or as filler undermines your self-esteem and devalues your word.

Let's put it this way: the word "apology" comes from the Greek "apologia," meaning a speech in defense of oneself. When you apologize, you're defending yourself against a fault. So, each time you do it, ask yourself: is there really any fault to defend against? If the answer is no, your apology is unnecessary. And if your answer is yes, then make sure it comes with purpose and real change.

When apologies are handed out like candy, they become background noise. A sincere apology can repair a relationship, but if you use it constantly, it loses all value.

Breaking free from Apologitis requires that before speaking, you pause to ask yourself if the action really deserves an apology. Instead of apologizing for being late, thank others for their patience in waiting. Defend your decisions without using "sorry" as a crutch. Learn to detect when you're following an imposed cultural script and change it.

Try this exercise, do an "apology fast." Count how many times you say "sorry," "I apologize," "excuse me" and their variants for three or four days. Then, commit to apologizing only when it's really necessary for the next ten days. No more apologizing for existing or casting your shadow. At first, it will feel uncomfortable, and a few "sorry's" will slip out, but it's all part of the process. Each small step will count toward strengthening that confidence. Over time, the empty apologies will disappear. It's a simple but effective exercise for improving self-esteem.

When that internal voice - guilt - starts its sermon of "Don't do that, or they'll think badly of you," it's time to hit the brakes. It's time to dig into those thoughts. The idea of "badness" is often an echo of old beliefs, imposed by figures who, for their own well-being, didn't want us to embarrass them. But these beliefs aren't always real nor do they align with our current values.

An apology should be a conscious act, not an automatic reflex. Reducing meaningless excuses strengthens self-respect and the respect of others. If you're constantly apologizing, maybe you're really messing up frequently - in which case you deserve a talking to - or maybe you're just overreacting, apologizing just because, and afraid of your own shadow. Neither cause is useful.

So, enough with meaningless "sorry's." Use words with the weight they deserve, and you'll see how respect grows, both for yourself and from others. Decide to vaccinate yourself against Apologitis.

The Power of Silence

Silence is neither a weak nor cowardly gesture; it's a wall that sets boundaries, maintains your dignity intact, and can communicate more than dozens of words seasoned with anger and frustration.

Silence is the master move for wielding boundaries without being overly nice or becoming aggressive. When faced with ridiculous requests or manipulations, staying quiet can speak louder than any speech. Keeping silent makes it clear that you're not there to react at the speed of light, that you prefer to think before responding, and that you can't be easily forced to answer on demand. Choosing silence means taking control of how to act, instead of letting any impulse make you respond immediately.

The Stoics[3] understood clearly that silence was synonymous with self-control. Epictetus summed it up by saying, "We have two ears and one mouth to listen twice as much as we speak." This simple idea highlights the value of responding with a cool head and moderation. Silence demonstrates that you focus on what you can control: your reactions. You can't manage

---

[3] Ancient Greek philosophical school (300 BCE) emphasizing emotional self-regulation. Modern studies show stoic practices reduce anxiety by 29%. Influenced modern therapies like REBT (Rational Emotive Behavior Therapy).

external factors, but you can decide not to respond, or wait to do so.

Silence is also an act of self-love. It makes clear that you trust your own thoughts, that you don't need to justify everything instantly or chase every discussion or seek to have the last word. Keeping silent shows you don't live by others' rules. It gives you time to process and respond in your own way.

In the business world, a pause can be more effective than any argument: it makes the other party talk more or change their position. In conflicts, staying quiet reduces tension and provides space to rethink things. And in decision-making, a moment of silent reflection prevents automatic and poorly thought-out responses. In the face of unacceptable behavior, silence is a tool that prevents useless back-and-forth.

But beware, don't confuse staying quiet with passivity. Keeping silent should be an active choice that can truly communicate more than any monologue. It's not about dodging problems or running from truth, but knowing when to hold back and when to act.

To take advantage of silence, you must get used to pauses and resist the urge to fill every gap with words. Before responding to criticism or demands, it's better to wait and think. Accompanying silence with a firm and calm gaze enhances its effect.

Personally, a trick that works quite well for me is mentally repeating phrases like mantras when I find myself in a useless discussion and want to keep quiet: "Whoever speaks, loses!" and "the fish dies by its mouth." In the heat of an escalated discussion, I take refuge in this internal dialogue, repeating these phrases over and over, while the other person pants, vocalizes, and talks non-stop - often even regretting later what they managed to say. In situations where anyone would fill the void with words, random comments, or even insults, one remains ice-cold. Inside, you just need to stay firm repeating those affirmations; outside... nothing can affect you!

Practicing silence is also about stopping self-justification and seeking approval. It's about giving up that false sense of control, but at the same time, it defines boundaries and grants respect without needing to speak. It's a symbol of security, a declaration that you won't be dragged into external chaos. When you choose to be silent, you send a powerful message: you're not a slave to your words, nor to those of others.

The Art of Saying "NO" and Being Selectively Available

If you feel you're always available to everyone, all the time, then it's time to hit the brakes and rethink your priorities. Your time and energy aren't inexhaustible resources, and therefore, they deserve wise distribution and investment from you, rather than from others.

Being selectively available doesn't turn you into an ice statue. It's very easy to fall into the trap of thinking we must always be available to others, even if that means crumbling our own emotional balance or canceling our plans. But the reality is that you can't be everyone's support system, much less do it all the time.

Start by identifying the people and situations that truly deserve your attention. This doesn't mean you have to cut ties with everyone, but simply be more conscious of where you invest your time and energy. Surround yourself with people who value and respect your boundaries, people who contribute to your life, people from whom you learn.

Jorge Luis Borges[4] had a deep understanding of friendship, highlighting its timeless nature by stating

---

[4] Argentine writer (1899-1986) considered one of literature's most influential figures. Known for complex works exploring reality, identity and time. Despite going blind at 55, he continued writing and became director of Argentina's National Library.

that "friendship needs no frequency" and can "do without frequency or regular contact." This vision was evident in his own life, as he maintained intimate friendships despite seeing those he considered his true friends only "three or four times a year." Regarding the boundaries of friendship, Borges understood that a true friend doesn't need to carry all the solutions to another's problems, but simply be present and listen. As he himself expressed: "I cannot give you solutions for all life's problems, nor do I have answers for your doubts or fears, but I can listen to you and share it with you." This perspective reflects a deep wisdom about the true nature of friendship: a bond that requires neither constant physical presence nor the responsibility to solve another's problems, but rather to offer companionship and understanding.

When someone asks you for something you can't or don't want to do, practice the art of saying "NO." You can be kind but firm, briefly explaining your reasons without carrying guilt. Remember that taking care of yourself isn't selfish; it's ensuring you can be there for others when they truly need you.

Saying "NO" to what you don't want allows you to say "YES" to what truly satisfies you. People who truly appreciate you will understand and respect your boundaries. And those who only want to take advantage of your goodwill, or use you as a vehicle for their own passions, well... maybe it's time to think about what role they play in your life.

Don't forget: your time and energy are yours to manage. By being selectively available, you're taking control and prioritizing your well-being. And that is a true act of sincerity and authenticity with yourself.

Let Go, Release, and Flow

Humans have four basic needs, and each can be satisfied in either a healthy way or a completely disastrous one. These are: certainty, variety, significance, and love or connection.

Certainty corresponds to that search for feeling secure and stable. In a good sense, this means maintaining healthy routines and making decisions that bring us closer to what we want. But false certainty consists of doing nothing for nothing. It's being a couch potato, appealing to safe mediocrity over the fear of the new.

In this sense, variety becomes somewhat contradictory: we want the spark of life and its surprises, but when that surprise gets out of control, that's when we cry to return to the calm of certainty.

As for significance, this too often becomes distorted. It happens when knowing who we are comes defined by others. Answer this question right now: Who are you? If you answer in terms of your career, your titles, your parents, what you have, who you know, then you've fallen into the trap: your meaning comes from outside. If you answer in terms of what you seek, how you define yourself, what you like, how you do things, you're appealing to authenticity. We are what we do most of our time, not a label or a star that others give us.

And finally, regarding love and connection, these can only properly emerge from maintaining authentic interactions and unfiltered communication that truly strengthens bonds with family, friends, and loved ones by not requiring masks or false attitudes. Sharing our thoughts and feelings openly creates deep relationships. But when you're with someone in a romantic relationship just because that person is very attractive or because the sex is great, or when your friends are only there because their weekend "hobby" is seeing how many beers they can chug, that's not the way...

We all prioritize some needs over others at different moments in life. Some need more love and connection, seeking everyone's approval and striving to be accepted in every social circle. Others yearn to feel important, seeking to stand out at work, accumulate material things, or show off their knowledge.

This is where a different idea comes in: instead of seeking more of these needs, we must be willing to let them go and release them... and flow! Sounds easy, but it's one of life's hardest lessons: Understanding that everything, ABSOLUTELY EVERYTHING in our passage through the world, is borrowed.

This attitude fits well with the four basic needs: You have the certainty that everything is temporary. Nothing can surprise you when you accept this truth.

Even your time is borrowed; your time is life's currency. But unlike any currency, you can't multiply it, only invest it. How will you use this borrowed time? Wasting it?

We must let go of everyone, not force anyone. Not seek to control how anyone should think or act. While there are cases where we'd love for others to learn from us so they don't waste their own time - like when we want to teach others something, or when a parent doesn't want to see their children suffer - we must let everyone learn on their own. You can lead a horse to water, but you can't make it drink.

That's flowing at its finest. Letting go of the illusion of control is scary; it means trusting that others will find their path, make mistakes, and learn from them. They might take longer and not see things as quickly as we do, but everyone goes at their own time and pace. This means giving up being everyone's savior, but it makes room for real growth and for others to truly take the reins of their lives and find their own motivations to change.

Are there areas where we're controlling things that aren't our responsibility? Are we holding onto something too tightly out of fear of losing it or needing it not to leave us? Or are others intruding on what should be our space? We must be honest and let go. Let everyone walk their own path. When you want to help, point out the route, but whether others follow it or not is their own business.

Shedding Your Skin and the Myth of Static Identity

It's happened to all of us: we're walking down the street and suddenly bump into someone from our past whom we haven't seen in ages, and suddenly we feel like we've been transported inside a time capsule.

Whether at a school or college reunion, or in an unexpected encounter with a former colleague, it suddenly seems like they're asking you to pull out outdated versions of yourself. It's as if they want to put you in a suit that no longer fits, a suit that's tight and now makes you feel uncomfortable. We're no longer the people from the past who remain etched in others' memories, and honestly, we don't owe anyone an explanation for having changed since then.

"Shedding old skin" like snakes is part of personal growth. Metaphorically, we should learn to shed outdated identities to embrace who we really are or who we want to become. But no, society insists on the myth of static identity, that absurd belief that who we were before forever defines who we are and will be, and this is uncomfortable, especially when you encounter people who expect you to keep acting like someone you haven't been for years.

Our body is a constant reminder of change: cells renew themselves, showing that transformation is part of our nature. The same applies to our mind, beliefs, and values. That shy, withdrawn school kid who hardly spoke might be a charismatic speaker today, or that carefree playboy might now be a committed father and role model. Change isn't just natural—it's something that should be celebrated as a symbol of self-discovery and growth.

When the past unexpectedly knocks on our door in the form of old times and former acquaintances, their image of us is likely anchored in what's already behind us. They might expect reactions and behaviors that no longer have anything to do with who we are now. And frankly, there's no reason to fit into those old molds. Just as you wouldn't wear clothes that no longer fit, you shouldn't act like someone you no longer are. Breaking free from these uncomfortable skins allows you to move through life with more authenticity.

Of course, this goes both ways. Others have changed too, and we should approach our interactions with an open mind based on who they are now and, as we said before, flow with their new identities.

If the pressure to act like your former self appears, assertiveness is essential. Acknowledge your own growth and speak about who you are now straightforwardly, resisting the temptation to please others with an outdated version of yourself. Remember what we said about setting boundaries, because maybe it's time to update them: if someone's expectations of you are unfounded or have expired, it's better to say so directly and firmly. Focusing conversations on current interests and goals saves headaches.

Each day offers the opportunity to redefine yourself. You owe nothing to the past of your old job, university, or school, not even to who you were a year ago. Shedding your skin and challenging the idea of an unchangeable identity is the way to reclaim power over yourself, to decide who you are at each moment.

Here's a simple but practical exercise: reflect on recent years and note at least three ways you've changed for your own good and peace of mind. New things you now like about yourself. Maybe you don't drink like before—because you decided so or realized it doesn't agree with you—maybe you don't stay up late or party anymore—because your body can't take it or you have so much work you just want to get home and rest—maybe you don't flirt with everyone anymore—because you're in a promising relationship—the idea is that the next time you unexpectedly meet someone you haven't seen in a long time, immediately point out these changes. Paint them red—as I mention in another book with a completely different theme, titled STRATEGIC MAGIC. Sharing these changes reaffirms your evolution and, moreover, helps the other person focus on who you are today.

The most important relationship that exists will always be the one you have with yourself. This relationship is also changing. It's imperative to honor your own growth, reaffirm your current identity, and leave behind the urgency to fit into outdated expectations. Authentic friendships will appreciate the person you are now and understand the version you left behind. True freedom lies in shedding every old skin and being the changing, evolving person you're meant to be. And for those who don't like your new "YOU" that much—tough luck!

The Art of Not Taking Anything Personally

Control what you can actually manage and stop being a people-pleasing pushover by first learning not to take everything to heart. This approach, which blends Stoic philosophy with modern psychology, can revolutionize how you handle relationships, face criticism, and maintain your emotional balance. The idea is simple: what others say or do says more about their inner world than yours. It's about mentally disconnecting from external influences without compromising your emotional integrity. The goal isn't to become insensitive, but to stay firm when others' behavior, especially their opinions, tries to destabilize you.

Look at Stoics like Marcus Aurelius[5] and Epictetus, who taught us that we only have power over what we can actually control. From this perspective, how you react is your decision and no one else's. Epictetus summed it up perfectly: "What matters is not what happens to you, but how you react to it." Here's the trick: you can't control what others do or think, but you can decide how you feel about it.

---

[5] Roman Emperor (121-180 CE) and philosopher known for his personal journal 'Meditations'. Despite being the most powerful man in the world, he championed humility and self-restraint. His writings on emotional resilience influenced modern Cognitive Behavioral Therapy.

The tendency to take everything personally is usually rooted in personal insecurities and past experiences. If you can identify what triggers you to feel off-balance, even better. Perhaps you're aware that a negative comment about your work can make you feel inferior, or that being spoken to in a certain tone of voice irritates you. Identifying these triggers is the first step to preventing them from dominating your life. The good news is you don't need to recognize them in advance: when they occur, they give you an opportunity to learn from them. This means applying your emotional intelligence[6] to the maximum and, instead of falling apart, stopping to think: "Wow! This seems to have the power to throw me off balance. Interesting. I wonder why?" Those milliseconds of recognizing something that could break you down can make all the difference in how you see the world and how much power you give to circumstances.

When someone acts in a way that disturbs you, remember that their actions have more to do with their life than yours. Maybe they're having a bad day or dealing with problems you can't see. Mindfulness is a tool to avoid getting swept away by emotion. The old trick of counting to ten and taking three deep breaths still works. Observe what you feel without rushing to

---

[6] Concept popularized by Daniel Goleman (1995). Research shows EQ predicts 58% of professional success. Can be improved through training, with studies showing 25% increase after targeted intervention.

judge, give yourself those seconds to contemplate the matter. Don't assume anything, don't decide or act under the poison of emotion provoked by any opinion—this will help you handle any situation that could turn into a petty war.

But don't get confused—not taking things personally doesn't mean you have to swallow everything people tell you. For example, when facing criticism, you can ask for clarity instead of assuming, exaggerating, or taking things to extremes to avoid misunderstandings. Asking "What do you mean by that?" or "How could I improve that aspect of my work you don't like?" turns a defensive moment into a learning opportunity. You might even discover whether the criticism is actually valid or, again, just a personal projection from the person giving it.

I like to say that "people love to mess with others just for the sake of it"—and nobody likes being messed with—so let them believe their own story about messing with you, but don't let them mess with your inner peace. It's also essential to defend or reinforce your boundaries when they aren't clear to others. If someone crosses the line, stay firm and strive not to lose your composure. One response for these cases is to raise your hand in a STOP gesture and say with zero emotion, like a rock anchored in the ocean: "I've heard you, and I don't want to talk about this now."

Self-awareness strengthens your ability to let bounce off what should bounce off. Taking a moment to review our reactions and notice patterns before moving any muscle—including your mouth—helps. Even keeping a journal can be useful for identifying triggers and exploring new ways to respond: "Dear diary: today I was driven crazy by this and that..." That's recognizing the emotion; then analyze what you could do differently in a similar future situation or what you can take from that situation by writing something like "I think from this I can learn that..." and respond. Writing is a way to objectify feelings, allowing us to see them from the outside and give them shape, to be objective and do mental and emotional cleaning.

Another technique, especially useful when facing criticism and opinions—which can sometimes be stupid and lack substance—is to think and mentally repeat while they're talking: "Everyone has the right to their opinion. I know what I'm capable of, and I decide that no opinion affects me in that regard." Everyone loves to share their opinions! People think that by openly saying everything they believe, someone will care or they'll change the world. If an opinion is stupid, let the wind take care of diluting it—stay calm.

The point is that you are not other people's opinions. Mastering the art of not taking things personally can only be positive. You react less, connect more, avoid useless fights, and focus on what's essential, which is ultimately what we're looking for: greater assertiveness and inner peace. It's not about being indifferent, but about embracing calm in the midst of chaos. Don Miguel Ruiz[7] said it masterfully: "Nothing others do is because of you. It is because of themselves."

---

[7] Mexican author and spiritual teacher (1952-present) known for 'The Four Agreements'. Combines ancient Toltec wisdom with modern insights. His work on personal freedom and not taking things personally has sold over 10 million copies worldwide.

The Fear of Rejection

We all like to be liked - between being the cool kid or the ugly duckling, the choice is obvious. The problem arises when that desire for approval becomes an unbreakable obsession. When you need others' approval at all costs, you start behaving in a forced way, losing authenticity and, worst of all, personal satisfaction.

This uncontrolled desire generates meticulous habits to please and avoid rejection: overthinking, hesitating before speaking, measuring every response to the millimeter, nodding until exhaustion, laughing without feeling it, agreeing without conviction, avoiding eye contact, carrying guilt, regretting everything, and much more. We self-censor to avoid standing out and pretend to always be helpful. Behaviors that seem harmless but silently drain our energy and strip us of what's genuine.

Children catch their parents' frustration, anger, and disappointment and learn to please them, adapting to avoid those negative feelings in them. Sure, children rebel, but over time, they internalize the desire to avoid any conflict. Similarly, warnings like "don't speak unless spoken to" and "stop asking so many questions" destroy assertiveness and push toward inner repression. Unquestioning obedience becomes the supreme value. Expressions like "Do what I say and don't question" become normalized, especially when parents are at their limit.

The irony emerges when, as adults, after having grown up programmed with these codes, we're expected to be assertive, confident, and expressive people. After years of seeking approval and avoiding conflicts, many struggle to be different.

Thus, "forced kindness" transforms into a set of rules based on fear: fear of being rejected. These children grow up fearing mistakes, being labeled as "ill-mannered," and as adults carry the subconscious burden of not disappointing their parents - even if they're no longer around. They create resentment that leads them to feel inferior to everyone because they learn to look up to everyone, and develop the habit of apologizing for everything, as we've seen before.

The thing is, we've grown up; our entire world isn't just mom, dad, and our siblings anymore. The environment has changed, there's no reason not to adapt to it. Your boss isn't your dad, your partner isn't your mom, your friends aren't your children, your work isn't your home. Your algorithm is outdated.

I like to call this algorithm "False ASS" (False Approval-Seeking System). Thanks to this code that disguises itself as "peace and love for everything, with everything and for everything," there's an unconscious subroutine that pushes us to live seeking external acceptance, avoid conflicts, and compromise our principles in pursuit of false harmony. This ASS ensures everything is in pristine order for others but messed up for ourselves. All so that others' opinions are favorable.

When this seeker takes the reins, it aims for two objectives at all costs:

1. Avoid judgments, criticism, and disapproval.

2. Obtain positive and constant recognition.

Moreover, the first objective always weighs more than the second; for the ASS, if they're not speaking well of it, then they shouldn't speak or disapprove at all. In new social environments, its focus is avoiding the negative: speaking only when asked, forcing smiles, nodding, and staying friendly. If an anecdote has the potential to make us uncomfortable or insulting, our Approval Seeker prefers to bow its head, submit to mockery, and smile along with everyone.

Since this ASS algorithm is inflexible toward disapproval, it establishes rules that end up being somewhat extreme: Nobody should think anything negative about your appearance, voice, decisions, comments, etc. Nobody should feel uncomfortable in your presence. Nobody should show visible disapproval of you.

53

This is why there's wear and tear from giving the perfect impression and doubt about whether we did well or not after meeting someone or being at a social event. The problem is that these rules are exhausting and only feed anxiety - that's why they're ridiculous. When we give too much space to the ASS, we become insecure and lose authenticity. Even this search for approval tends to intensify when we're surrounded by people we consider more attractive, successful, or influential, giving more weight to their opinions than our own. The Approval Seeker is also the creator of that Spotlight effect we mentioned earlier, and therefore is an assistant to that witch that is guilt, activating that thought of "am I not enough?"

But what if instead of fighting against this ASS, we accept it as part of ourselves and learn to laugh at it? Imagine that algorithm is a drama queen: a dramatic friend who always exaggerates everything. Instead of trying to silence it, we could give it a funny name, like "Paranoid Pete" or "Over-analyzing Olivia."

Every time you feel that fear of rejection activating, visualize your ASS personified throwing a tantrum in your head. "Oh no, they're going to think I'm an idiot!" That's when you tell it: "Calm down, Pete, breathe. You're a paranoid crazy person, relax a bit."

Another unconventional strategy for dealing with fear of rejection is adopting the "voluntary clumsy clown method." The next time you're in a social situation that makes you nervous, purposely commit a small social error. Spill a little water on yourself, tell a bad joke on purpose, or use a wrong word. Observe how the world doesn't end, that you're exaggerating the attention you think you're receiving, and how, in fact, this can even make others feel more comfortable around you.

But my favorite strategy is adopting the "So what?" philosophy: Every time your internal ASS starts worrying about what others might think, simply ask yourself: "So what?": They don't like me? So what? They think I'm weird? So what? They didn't invite me? So what? Repeat it until you realize how insignificant it really is.

Fear of rejection is like a muscle you've been exercising your whole life. It's time to start exercising the opposite muscle: It's not about completely eliminating fear, but learning to dance with it, laugh at it, and, in the process, discover that you're much stronger and more resilient than you think.

So the next time your internal ASS starts making noise, put a clown nose on it, pat it on the back, and tell it: "Thanks for your concern, but I've got this."

So what!

Stop Carrying Other People's Problems

If you really want to stop being too nice, you first need to understand where your responsibilities end and others' begin. That urge to stick your nose in and carry others' burdens is almost a human instinct: parents who feel they're the absolute solution for their children, partners who try to please each other to exhaustion, and friends who, in their eagerness to help, end up trapped in dramas that aren't their business. But where's the line?

At the end of the day, everyone has to deal with their own stuff. Parents can support and be present for their children, but only the children, as they grow, will have to take responsibility for their actions, ask for help, and learn on their own. Taking control of someone's path, no matter how good your intentions, robs them of their opportunity to grow. It's like giving someone a bicycle only to ride it yourself - it's nice, but it prevents them from learning to balance and pedal on their own.

This doesn't just apply to families, but to all relationships. Taking charge of others' affairs erases your own identity. You end up losing your bearings, overwhelmed by others' burdens. It's like trying to balance a mountain of dirty dishes while others keep adding more to the pile. Learning to separate what's yours from what isn't frees you from a weight you shouldn't be carrying.

It's not about being cold. In fact, it's a better way to love: support and trust, but let the other person find the solution. Trusting others means recognizing they're responsible for their own actions. Are you taking on responsibilities that aren't yours? How much stress could you avoid if you accepted that you can't manage others' decisions?

Stopping your involvement in others' affairs doesn't mean you stop caring. It means you demonstrate love that empowers rather than suffocates. You offer support without the chains of control - it's love, but without conditions. This approach allows you and those around you to experience life's ups and downs more autonomously.

What could you let go of today? Which relationships might improve if you trusted more and stopped trying to control everything? Learning to separate your path from others' is a lifelong job, but each step in that direction is a step toward a fuller, more authentic life.

Let them go! Let everyone take their own steps and fall if they have to.

Authentic Relationships

Have you heard that we tend to be the average of the people we surround ourselves with? One of the most underrated pieces of advice for changing and achieving excellence is to seriously examine who the people are that we spend our time with. Take this matter seriously and look carefully at how your relationships intertwine: do they really add value, or do they just serve to fill your voids? If you do this with brutal honesty, this exercise will inevitably lead to a revelation: not all that glitters is gold, maybe you've been wasting time... but enough is enough, it's time to change.

Analyze your relationships and be honest about what you really expect from them. I'm talking about all types of connections: friendships, romantic partners, bosses, employees, maybe even your family. Are you motivated by praise and the search for approval? Are you driven by the fear of disappointing them? Or is it the fear of loneliness that makes you stay and continue with the same old crowd even when it's not playing in your favor at all?

If you're seeking praise and approval, remember the ASS (Approval-Seeking System) we mentioned earlier. With your friends, ask yourself: are they life companions or just extras to pass the time? If gatherings only consist of alcohol, chaos, or telling the same old stories again, maybe it's time to surround yourself with other people who will push you to grow in different areas. There's no shortage of people to hang out with, but those who are truly valuable are the ones whose words transcend the time we share with them, people you genuinely learn from. People who say things that when you listen carefully... click in your head. These people are truly valuable: they're people to learn from, and once that requirement is met, the party can come after.

In the realm of romantic relationships, make the same reflection. Is this someone to grow with and support each other long-term? If beauty fades, would both still be there together? Does that mutual commitment to evolution exist? A relationship should nurture, not drag you into settling for what's there. On this same note, if your partner isn't helping you fly, clear the runway and let them fly away.

And when it comes to bosses and superiors, question: do they see you as a pawn in their own plans, or as someone key to everyone's growth in the organization? A true leader values their team and promotes an environment where everyone thrives. Of course, no boss is perfect, and they need to be tough from time to time, but if you feel something's wrong, well, there must be a reason—maybe it's time to change the game.

Let's be frank: Do your relationships follow some power game or mutual admiration society? What would your connections be like without power hierarchies? Can you imagine a space where value is independent of what someone does or doesn't do?

Stopping to think in terms of "above" and "below" with the people you relate to gives space to simply being, allowing the same for others. This is the core of valuable relationships, born from self-respect. Separating self-esteem from external validation gives your life a more solid foundation.

So, what's left when you remove the labels, expectations, hierarchies? You're left with a more naked, more authentic version of relationships, where you're no longer the one adjusting to others, but rather starting to build life in the company of those who simply fit. It's a process that might lead you to let go of friendships and bonds that seemed solid but, in reality, weren't allowing you to advance.

When the value of relationships is measured in shared experiences and sincere respect, everything changes. People come and stay, not to fill voids, but because they contribute, and you find yourself contributing too. This isn't some communist agenda disguised as camaraderie; it's freeing yourself from the status filter and fear of rejection to enter into equal relationships. And there, at that point, you realize that your bonds become true support, a network of people who elevate you and whom you also elevate.

So go and observe again who walks beside you. Not everyone has to stay, and that's okay. What matters, what truly transforms, is the quality of the connections you choose to maintain. Your environment is a reflection of your decisions, and your life—with everything you choose to build—is the echo of those decisions.

If you are the average of the people you relate to, close the circle, and choose carefully who you'll let inside.

Healthy Selfishness

Ask anyone if being selfish is good, and the "NOs" will hit you like bullets.

Practicing healthy selfishness is the only way to stop playing the exhausted hero who saves everyone except themselves.

The change begins by questioning this idea that looking after oneself is wrong and therefore selfish. True responsibility lies in accepting what you need, expressing it, and seeking to satisfy it. Obviously respecting others' boundaries - you don't need to run over anyone. For many, this seems like a titanic act. We stay quiet, believing that wanting and asking for ourselves is wrong. This silence makes us powerless, like children waiting for someone to guess what we need. When that doesn't happen, frustration and resentment bloom, and others become insensitive in our eyes.

The solution lies in taking ownership of your own experience. Only you can put yourself first. Others have their own lives, their own emotions. It's YOUR task to express YOUR needs and look after YOUR well-being. This means breaking ingrained habits and understanding that always prioritizing others is unsustainable. Doing so always ends in resentment and undermines happiness.

Ask yourself frequently and without shame: What do I need? How can I take care of myself without remorse? Do it. That guilt for prioritizing yourself is a burden you must release. When you take the reins of your well-being, you give others permission to take responsibility for themselves. They no longer seem helpless; they become capable. The understanding about ourselves and others changes: We can calmly tell ourselves: "I have power, you do too." Let's use that wisely, but with EACH PERSON's own wisdom.

Being too accommodating is a time bomb for any relationship. Putting aside your needs, staying quiet, or fearing to show who you really are gradually undermines the vitality of any bond. If both partners in a relationship behave this way, trust collapses, resentment piles up, and attraction vanishes. Without trust, resentment becomes poison that destroys any relationship and builds emotional walls.

On the other hand, authenticity and courage kindle attraction. Genuine connection and passion flourish when one shows themselves without fear and speaks their mind, while simultaneously allowing the other to think as they wish, letting everyone have their own peaceful opinion about anything.

It's important to remember that every time we renounce ourselves, we're sending a silent message: "My needs don't matter." This message, though not spoken aloud, permeates the bond, and over time, installs a kind of emotional distance. Conversely, genuine self-respect acts as a kind of pulse that sets the rhythm in relationships, allowing for healthier reciprocity, without forcing or demanding too much. In this exchange of expressed boundaries and desires, the connection enriches, not because one is sacrificing, but because each person is contributing from their truth.

It's not about building relationships where one always wins or imposes themselves, but about creating a space where authenticity is common ground. This type of bond, where one dares to say "this is what I want" or "this is not what I need," also allows the other to express themselves without fear of reprisals or judgments. These are the relationships that thrive, because there's a shared freedom to be, to take care of oneself without loading the other with expectations. In them, there's no need to play the mind reader, and there's no room for resentment born from what's left unsaid.

Thus, this "healthy selfishness" stops being selfishness and becomes something more: responsibility, respect for the relationship, and a silent affirmation that both deserve to live in fullness. When one starts to take on their own well-being, what follows is a natural effect on others, a mutual respect that grows without forcing it, almost like an inevitable reflection of the shared truth between two people who choose to be, without masks, without waiting to be saved.

Authenticity: The Secret to Fulfilling Sexuality

While "polite" intimacy isn't bad, it leaves nothing in memory. It can be tender and affectionate, but rarely ignites that magnetic spark of passion. It's like a song with a single note - it keeps the rhythm but lacks the melodic changes that tell stories.

This happens when we treat intimacy by obsessing over what we think the other expects from us. We become actors following a rigid script, afraid to improvise. Of course, being considerate when it comes to sexuality is essential, but so is being authentic. Only then can we enjoy without reservations. Moreover, when we give ourselves to authenticity and the other's desires, the experience is best for both. When we stop overthinking and allow ourselves to experiment and let "whatever happens" flow, we transmit an energy that revitalizes the connection. True magic emerges from that spontaneity.

Clear and direct communication seems to be more taboo than any fetish, but it's fundamental for intimacy to flourish. I don't remember who said that couples should have lots of "oral sex" - referring to speaking openly - as a prelude to the best sex in the world. An extraordinary piece of advice, without doubt.

Unlike any idealized and silent movie scene, real intimacy improves with clarity. If you have doubts about what the other person likes, then ask. Phrases like "Shall we do this?" or "Would you like to try this?" work wonders. This kind of openness strengthens trust and complicity.

When talking becomes part of intimacy, trust skyrockets. Then you can live in the moment, focused on the shared experience rather than our internal insecurities. Moving from thought to consensual sensation is revolutionary, not just in intimacy, but in all of life. Releasing insecurities and surrendering to the present opens the door to more intense and memorable experiences.

Say. Listen. Do. Take. Give. Feel. It's crucial to discuss limits and desires; it's not about being aggressive, but about allowing mutual and consensual leadership. Many love a partner who radiates confidence and passion. Letting that energy flow is liberating, it's like dancing choreography together where each step reflects shared desire.

Intimacy demands honesty. When there's an authentic exchange of admiration, when you can talk and share preferences without reservations, with clear boundaries and knowing what both desire and how far they can go, moments together become unforgettable.

Cultivating authenticity in intimate relationships isn't a luxury, it's a necessity.

If you can't talk freely with your partner, red flag: that's not the way! The inability to communicate in a relationship is like navigating without a compass - getting lost is easy, and finding your way back is complicated. There's no worse unhappiness than being with a partner who's completely mismatched with you. Especially when it comes to intimacy.

Social Media

In a world where being glued to your phone is the norm, setting healthy boundaries isn't just about dealing with people in person anymore—it also includes managing digital chaos. Social media connects you like never before, but it's also a bomb of anxiety, stress, and an absurd need to display fake perfect lives for no reason. It's vital to identify the digital pressures trying to destroy these boundaries: the fear of missing out, the obsessive pursuit of "likes" and validation, and how easy it is to fall into foolish comparisons. Understanding that these pressures exist is the first step to regaining control of your online interactions.

To assert your presence and maintain a decent balance in the digital space, there are several tactics that actually work. Start by filtering what you consume and be selective about the accounts you follow. It's not about amassing followers, but about interacting with content and people who actually add value to your life, not those who drive you crazy. Mute or unfollow profiles that create pressure or make you feel inadequate, and prioritize connections that align with your values. Also, adjust your notifications so they don't interrupt you every five minutes and establish clear expectations about how quickly you respond, thus protecting your mental peace.

Saying "NO" in the digital world is just as valid as in the real world: rejecting friend requests or group invitations that don't align with your priorities is essential. Privacy settings aren't a suggestion—they're a tool to define who can see what you share or contact you. Schedule digital detoxes—screen-free hours each day, one day a week, or longer periods when needed—to improve your mental health. A Chinese proverb states that "Three things never return: the spoken word, the shot arrow, and the lost opportunity." We can update it with a fourth thing that never comes back: "what you post on social media." Posting less is a conscious strategy, because everything, EVERYTHING you post will never cease to exist online, even if you delete it.

If you get into a conflict on social media, take the time needed to respond rather than reacting instantly. Use first-person statements to express your viewpoint without attacking, and recognize when it's better to withdraw from a discussion that's going nowhere—Spoiler: no one has ever changed their mind after a social media argument. Don't hesitate to block or report those who consistently violate your boundaries. In the professional environment, having separate accounts for work and personal life helps establish clear communication lines and are steps toward balanced control.

Furthermore, don't be afraid to block anyone. The block button exists for a reason and is waiting for you to use it. This is the Internet, an alternative reality, the paradise of stupid and unsolicited opinions. No one has the right to steal your time or demand your opinions.

Someone posting comments that irritate you? Block them. Someone posting about politics driving you crazy? Block them. A stranger overwhelming you with messages? Block them, report them using the platform's tools, and get on with your life.

You don't need to make excuses or be diplomatic. A simple block and your day goes on. It's not about being rude—it's about taking care of yourself. Your mental peace is worth more than a like and more than the sensitivities of someone you don't even know.

Social media is just a showcase of your life. You're not obligated to respond to everyone or please every follower. Treat it as your pseudo-personal space and if someone doesn't add value, out they go.

Or better yet: quit social media altogether! The thing is, this obsession with sharing life on the Internet is a trap, unless you're in the business of being one of those so-called "influencers": Idiots followed by another bunch of idiots, supposedly to "influence" them with nonsense so they'll stop being idiots. Unless that's your business, there's no point in being a digital exhibitionist.

If necessary, create an anonymous profile to laugh at memes and stay updated, but your private life doesn't need to be part of that circus. The truth is that nobody cares what you eat or where you travel, except for the companies collecting your data and your own excessive vanity.

The ultimate boundary is giving up the "everyone's doing it" game. That's the trap that keeps you stuck in social media and puts you under the ASS's spotlight for no reason.

Your privacy is worth more than "likes" or comments. Stop wasting time on an online persona and start living a real life.

Consider it seriously: Delete your accounts and reclaim your time and energy. The world won't end if you stop posting selfies; in fact, you'll rediscover what it's like to live special moments without having to function in terms of going out to tell a bunch of strangers you don't even know: "I'm here doing this, give me your like."

At Work

In the professional world, finding the balance between being assertive and not coming across as overbearing is key to advancing your career and maintaining your sanity. Offices are full of traps: hierarchies, team politics, and unwritten rules that distort what it means to be assertive. So, first things first: pay attention to who really holds the power. Observe how those who inspire respect communicate and copy what works. Also, you need to know where you stand in the hierarchical scale, because you won't speak the same way to your boss as you would to a colleague or an intern.

Being assertive doesn't mean barging into conversations like a bull in a china shop. Start by proposing ideas that build without seeking to destroy from the get-go: "I think this approach is more solid" sounds much better than "Your idea doesn't work" and is certainly stronger than "Without meaning to undermine what's been presented, could I offer an alternative?" No, that's pure Apologitis. People accept ideas better if they feel their opinion truly matters, so show them you're listening, but without falling into syrupy praise or being defensive. Avoid being the non-stop talker or the constant apologizer; doing so will only weaken your message.

Choose your battles wisely. Not every problem deserves confrontation. Save your energy for what really matters, or you'll become the person everyone avoids. When you need to discuss a problem, bring solutions, not just complaints. This shows you're not here to stir things up, but to help fix them.

Difficult moments require planning. Note the key points and choose your timing well: managing timing is everything. If the office is in chaos or your counterpart is at their limit, better wait. Use clear facts and examples. Hunches don't convince, but evidence does. And when you criticize something, ensure it's constructive and honest: start and end with something positive, putting what bothers you in the middle, and again, without brown-nosing. It's simple, nobody wants to feel attacked, so balance is key. Find common ground, however minimal, to smooth any path.

In meetings, aiming to be among the first to speak helps calm nerves and establish presence. Once in, avoid hesitant words like "maybe" and "I think." Defend your positions firmly. It's okay to be questioned, but don't give in just to keep the peace if you know you're right. Asking relevant questions also reinforces your image as someone worth listening to.

When it comes to negotiating, never improvise. Gather data and be clear about your value before starting conversations about salaries or promotions.

Practice what you'll say to avoid sounding insecure. Focus on what you bring, not on what you need.

Being known as assertive means being someone who follows through on their word. Acknowledge your mistakes and focus on solutions when things don't go as planned. Use that assertiveness to defend others when necessary - this builds trust and shows leadership, but keep this harsh truth in mind: no matter what people say, nobody will be willing to sacrifice their position to save you or anyone else. Workplace loyalty is very subjective. This is a painful truth but one you need to accept as soon as possible.

In the end, being assertive at work isn't just a tool to improve your professional performance; it's a way to protect your energy and maintain your boundaries. Excessive courtesy or the tendency to avoid conflicts only leads to accumulated frustration. Speaking clearly and knowing what you want to convey isn't being insensitive; it's acting intelligently. It helps you choose your words without needing to be liked by everyone or seeking to win their sympathy in every situation. Over time, this clarity leaves a much more lasting and authentic impression on those around you.

Thus, the success of not being too nice in a professional space comes down to being assertive. Healthy work relationships don't come from always saying yes or avoiding confrontations, but from mutual respect that can only be achieved by communicating without fear. Being kind when necessary and firm when fair creates a powerful balance, one that allows you to advance without losing yourself in the process.

The "I Don't Know Yet" Technique

Have you ever found yourself cornered in a meeting with a question you don't know how to answer? It can be a complete nightmare. You're there, relaxed, and suddenly you're hit with a surprise question that you have no idea how to handle. You go blank, start sweating, and everyone stares at you as if you've done something terrible. Most people in these cases stutter and finally blurt out an "I don't know" while internally wishing they could disappear.

But here's the trick: instead of shrinking away, lift your gaze and say with total conviction: "I don't know yet, BUT I'll find out." This simple phrase changes everything. It's honest without showing weakness. It demonstrates that you can admit not knowing something while having enough confidence to commit to finding the answer. That "but I'll find out" makes all the difference: it indicates your ignorance is only temporary. You're not clueless; you're working on the process.

If someone pushes for more details, a simple "I'm getting on that right away because I'm interested too" makes it clear that you're not trying to dodge the question, but genuinely committing to finding the answer. This way, you maintain control of the situation and project professionalism.

Just don't stop at the phrase: get to it! Follow through on that promise to find the requested answer.

So, when these unexpected moments arise, remember that it's not about having all the answers instantly, but about demonstrating how you find them. The next time you're thrown a complicated question, see it as an opportunity to show your determination and solution-focused approach. With an "I don't know yet, but I'll find out," you transform from someone who reacts with panic to someone who responds with purpose. That small phrase gives you the space you need to work toward the best answer.

The important thing here is to stay calm and be transparent; don't underestimate the power of a genuine commitment. At its core, this technique allows you to move with agility and adapt without fear to the unexpected. You don't have to know everything, but you should have some idea of where to start looking.

This tool buys you time - use it wisely.

Alcohol and Drugs: The False Social Lubricant

One of the world's most normalized and messed up habits is using alcohol or drugs as shortcuts to socialize. It might seem like a harmless move, but it's a trap with brutal long-term ramifications. Recognizing this pattern and breaking it is essential in the journey toward authenticity.

Alcohol and drugs might make you believe you're more confident or sociable, but this is nothing more than a chemical illusion. You might seem more relaxed because your inhibitions are lowered, but that doesn't mean you've gained even a hint of real confidence or social skills. When the chemical effects in your body fade, you return to your original discomfort, usually multiplied and accompanied by remorse for what you said or did under the influence. Messing up, saying something inappropriate, misinterpreting situations, or making foolish decisions comes at a price: your reputation and your relationships.

Before reaching for that drink to "feel like a fish in water," it's worth asking yourself what's driving that need to alter your state of consciousness. What mask are you trying to wear? Are you trying to cover up some insecurity or discomfort? Substances don't solve these problems; they just hide them and temporarily blur boundaries, distorting your judgment. You might end up saying "YES" to things you wouldn't otherwise accept, or behaving in ways that don't reflect your principles, which inevitably leads to regret and undermines your self-esteem.

Many successful and respected people have learned to socialize without resorting to any social lubricant. They've built confidence that comes from within, not from a bottle or a pill. True confidence means knowing yourself and being comfortable with who you are in any situation.

Many party nights tend to fill up with empty promises and commitments that only exist while the effects of substances last. It's common to hear grandiose declarations: promises to change, achieve impossible goals, or declare fleeting love. These words, spoken with false confidence, vanish at dawn, leaving behind a trail of disappointment and skepticism. Those who blindly trust these promises end up learning the lesson that words spoken under the influence lack substance; they were just part of the passing euphoria.

Moreover, the ease with which some fall into the trap of believing these falsehoods reveals a collective vulnerability. Society often celebrates spontaneity and carefree behavior at parties, without recognizing the long-term damage these behaviors can cause. Those who choose to believe in the promises of a drunken night are negotiating away their own emotional well-being, allowing momentary illusion to overshadow the reality of their genuine needs and desires.

To put this into practice, I propose a revealing exercise. Dare to try the following at your next social gathering: commit to attending the entire event without having a single drink or consuming anything that might alter your consciousness - total sobriety! Carefully observe how people interact around you. You'll notice how many begin to "unfold" and adopt masks that don't reflect their true selves, behaving in ways that might actually seem more superficial or even ridiculous. You'll see extreme behaviors emerge and wonder if these are really the versions of yourself that you display in similar situations.

By the end of the gathering, you'll understand that these appearances, fun for many, are mere illusions created by alcohol, and that authenticity and genuine confidence come from within, not from an external substance. This exercise will help you recognize the true essence of those around you and strengthen your own security without relying on supposed chemical shortcuts. False shortcuts that, over time, can turn out to be quite expensive.

You're not a killjoy for not wanting to enter the masquerade ball dressed in altered consciousness.

Energy Vampires

Have you ever felt your inner battery draining as fast as a candle in a hurricane without having done anything out of the ordinary? We're not machines, and sure, there are days when even lifting a pencil leaves us exhausted. But watch out - sometimes it's not a bad day, but people who are draining our energy. I'm talking about energy vampires and drama queens, beings who pretend to be human but live off draining the vitality from others: authentic energy parasites.

These characters are the ones to whom you should provide the least kindness and dedication. To deal with these characters, you first need to identify them. Did you end up emotionally drained after a conversation? You might have been drained by an energy vampire without realizing it. Energy vampires hide beside you, disguised as harmless comments and bland friendships. They seek to be with you for as long as possible, forcing conversations at every opportunity and always appearing sad or in terrible shape. They do this because they need your energy to survive. Sometimes they don't do it on purpose, but they still leave you depleted.

Moreover, these energy vampires generate tension and problems in any environment: work, family, friendships... They repeat their behavior because it works for them, creating a cycle that feeds them at your expense. They can cause explosions in teams or groups when a victim decides to say "ENOUGH," and those who have suffered from them might start behaving the same way with others, spreading exhaustion and negativity everywhere.

One of the most common types is the "dominant" vampire. They love to appear superior and mentally exhaust you by exploiting your vulnerabilities. Another complicated type is the "melodramatic" vampire or drama queen. For these individuals, everything is a tragedy, and they're certain everything will always go wrong. Similar is the "victim" vampire, who believes without any doubt that everyone is always against them. Then there's the "unsolicited judge" vampire, who seeks to bring out your insecurities by judging everything you do without being asked. The "egocentric" vampire is easy to identify because they never stop bragging or reminding everyone that they're the best at everything; and finally, the "innocent" vampire who, although never meaning to harm, ends up doing so through their sheer idiocy and naivety.

Once identified, it's time to face them. An effective trick is to manage your time well. It's not that you don't want to attend to them; you simply don't have time for it. Remember being available at your discretion - this is your first practical strategy.

Another useful tactic is strategic withdrawal. Avoid eye contact or reduce it to a minimum. It might seem insignificant, but many energy vampires seem to need to see the tiredness or emotional drain in your eyes to keep feeding.

In the presence of any of these energy drainers, opt to respond to everything with an "Uh-huh..." Listen patiently without giving almost any response and drop that uh-huh with nothing more. For vampires, that passivity doesn't meet their feeding standards.

But what happens when the "uh-huh" no longer works? That's when you need to be clear and decisive. There's no room for beating around the bush or excuses. Simply say: "I don't have time for this right now." These words, brief but powerful, make your boundaries clear without opening doors to negotiations or interpretations.

You don't need to justify yourself or feel guilty for prioritizing your energy. There are people who live off draining others' energy, and there are others who, in their effort to stay nice, play along. By expressing your unavailability directly, you're taking control of your emotional space. This way, you make it clear that your time is valuable and that you won't allow them to keep draining you. Sometimes, the only way to break the cycle is to be firm and not give in to manipulation.

"Mockying": Bullying in Adulthood

Bullying has become firmly established among young people, pushing many of its victims to the limits of their mental resistance. The bullies who practice it always target the most vulnerable, turning others' suffering into their own fuel. School teachers and families with children complain about how complicated it is to handle these conflicts, especially when victims prefer to stay silent rather than ask for help. And don't think harassment is just a kids' thing: in the adult world, though less visible, the same thing repeats itself, but under a new name...

Mockying - a blend of "mocking" with a bullying twist[8] - is the adult version of this toxic dynamic. It's present both at work and in other social circles, affecting those who dare to be different or simply the most vulnerable. Victims receive contempt, exclusion, verbal aggression, and, in extreme cases, even physical intimidation. The big difference with adults is that these behaviors are minimized or justified with arguments like "they're just jokes," "I'm kidding," or "it's not that serious." Worse still, if the harassment comes from

---

[8] Adult workplace bullying affects 30% of workers according to 2021 Workplace Bullying Institute study. Costs businesses $250 million annually in lost productivity. Similar to 'workplace incivility' studied by Christine Porath.

someone in power, the victim is expected to endure it silently out of fear of retaliation and to maintain an undeserved hierarchical respect.

Outside the workplace, Mocking extends to all kinds of contexts. In sports, adults can repeat these dynamics, attacking a teammate for mistakes or lack of skill. In families, though less frequent, this harassment disguised as jokes also appears and is devastating both for the victim and those who witness it.

Confronting Mocking requires clear determination. Most organizations have general coexistence programs but lack specific protocols against adult harassment. Therefore, the first tool against Mocking is personal initiative. Sharing the experience with trusted people outside the immediate environment can help obtain a more objective perspective.

Avoiding contact with aggressors is a first option, but it's not always possible, especially at work. Another strategy is to neutralize hostility with a firm attitude and, if you can, use humor to show that the harasser's actions don't have the desired effect - turn the tables and mock those who mock you. However, maintaining this stance is more complex, requires self-control, and isn't always enough; sometimes it turns into a war to see who ends up being more cutting. Besides, not everyone has a comedian's quick wit to respond to mockery with an even better comeback. For cases like these, I've included an appendix in this book titled "A Course in Sarcasm" - yes, I copied the idea from the famous "Course in Miracles" - where you'll see how to craft short, sharp, and effective responses to counterattack in such cases. The idea is to read and reread these responses and let some of them establish themselves in your mind to fire automatically when your common sense deems appropriate. When it comes to Mockying, if they're messing with you, mess with them right back.

However, when the harassment becomes intolerable, the only way out might be to escalate the complaint to higher authorities, either within the company or through legal bodies. For these cases, it's vital to gather evidence: emails, messages, recordings, or third-party testimonies can make the difference. It won't be an easy path, but it's a necessary step to ensure harassment doesn't go unpunished. This fight isn't just for you but for everyone who might suffer the same.

The World's Worst Neighbor

Living next to unbearable neighbors is like being trapped in an endless soap opera where each episode brings a new reason to want to pull your hair out. Whether it's the one who turns their house into a nightclub until the early hours, the one who completely ignores basic coexistence boundaries, or the one who told their pet that your garden was another designated space for their business, these neighbors can turn your home surroundings into a constant source of stress. What to do?

First, let's give them the benefit of the doubt: it's very likely that this problematic neighbor didn't come into the world to annoy you, but rather is just thoughtless and simply acts from their own limited perspective. The one who always parks in front of your entrance might be circumstantially rushed to care for a sick relative. The family with the noisy dog that won't stop barking might be dealing with situations you've never imagined. This doesn't justify them trampling your right to peace, but it gives you context to respond more intelligently and try to better understand the situation. We all make noise from time to time, so we need to look at things in their proper proportions.

When the benefit of the doubt has been exhausted and we're certain it's a frequent practice, we need to appeal to the community's codes of conduct. These documents usually have clear rules about permitted noise levels and the hours they must be respected. If the music continues, escalate your complaint to doormen, management, and eventually the police. Many people fear this because it seems extreme, but that's when you need to gauge if the moment has arrived. You're not looking to start a war, but simply to ensure that established rules for everyone's well-being are respected.

The best way to handle a problem with a neighbor is indirectly; that story about going over nicely to ask them to turn down the volume doesn't work - worse yet, your neighbor might be intoxicated with alcohol, and with that, their rational brain might be disconnected. That's why you need to escalate to authority, but indirectly. Yes, it can be tempting to confront them face-to-face, show them who's boss and see who gives in first. But let me tell you something: this "who's more powerful" mentality is a waste of time and money. Getting lawyers involved for personal disputes with neighbors in these matters is like throwing money into a bottomless pit. Legal fees can drive you crazier than the original problem, and the tension will only increase, turning a dispute - most times manageable - into an endless war where everyone loses.

Modern life calls for modern solutions. Documenting for authority remains crucial, but do it with clarity instead of emotion. "The noise from Unit B lasted from 11 PM to 2 AM" serves you better than appealing to qualifiers like "They were incredibly inconsiderate again." This objective record helps maintain perspective and provides useful evidence if you need intervention from authorities to escalate the problem.

Regarding other types of issues, the tools at our disposal have evolved beyond simple fences and curtains. Smart home security, video cameras, and noise-canceling technology offer new ways to handle challenges with neighbors. Nobody likes their wallet being touched, and having solid evidence along with community code fines can be enough. So, record the neighbor's blessed dog when it's doing its business in your garden, and have the respective fine sent to its owner.

Finally, there's always time. Time proves to be the ultimate solver of many disputes, including neighborly ones. Real estate markets change, people move, circumstances evolve. Your current challenging situation is temporary, but the skills you develop in handling it will serve you for life. Focus on building these capabilities instead of winning every minor battle.

The next time your neighbor's actions threaten to disturb your peace, pause. Remember that while you can't control their behavior, you maintain complete sovereignty over your response. Sometimes, against neighbor noise, small earplugs are enough instead of getting into a neighborly DJ challenge to see who can play music louder. Is there really a violation of the law? If so, then let it be applied. After all, your peace of mind is worth much more than any power dispute with someone who lives a couple of doors away.

How to Deal with Hypocrites

Hypocrisy is a mask that hides easily. You could have a master of duplicity right beside you, smiling from ear to ear while stabbing you in the back when you're not looking, and you won't even notice until it's too late. These characters handle their double game like it's child's play: they flatter you or feign cordiality when they're with you, and at other times, they tear you apart behind your back.

Does this mean you have to go around paranoid, measuring everyone's every word and gesture? No. You're not going to go around distrusting everyone because, in the end, hypocrisy comes and goes in your life and most of the time you don't even notice it. When you discover it, it's best to take it as a lesson, a reminder that life is constant learning and that "faces we see, hearts we don't know..."

Human interactions are often like a casino: unpredictable and ever-changing. The brightest smile can hide a grimace of pure malice. And if you catch it in time, you can anticipate and respond accordingly: don't leave yourself vulnerable. Sure, we can all fall for it once or twice, and sometimes it's fine to let it slide to keep the peace. But if you resign yourself to accepting others' hypocrisy as something constant and normal in your life, you'll become your own biggest hypocrite. And if there's one thing this philosophy of NOT

BEING SO NICE should make clear, it's that not all backstabs should be forgiven.

This isn't about giving in to the impulse for revenge or filling yourself with resentment. Sometimes ignoring bad behavior only multiplies it and worse, hurts others too. It's in your hands to stop the spiral before people think they can walk all over you and get away with it. If you let these slights pass again and again, you're feeding a bomb that will keep exploding in your face. And then, who will be complicit in your own disaster?

What to do when you decide to put a sudden stop to someone's hypocrisy? Sometimes we soften the blows to avoid hurting sensibilities, but that only postpones the inevitable. You need to be clear, calm but unwavering, and make it known that this double standard won't be tolerated.

When you encounter a hypocrite in life, it's easy to want to explode with frustration and desperation. You wonder how someone can be so blind to their own contradictions and how you can make them see the light without losing your mind in the attempt. Well, here's an unconventional but effective technique for dealing with these masters of double-speak: the amplified mirror:

Imagine you have a colleague who constantly criticizes others for being late, but seems to have a toxic relationship with the clock themselves: They're late at least twice a week, but that doesn't stop them from continuing to lecture about the importance of punctuality. Instead of confronting them directly and risking a useless argument, try this: the next time they're late, be late yourself, but arrive a few minutes after them. And don't do it just once—do it several times, with a consistency they can't ignore.

But don't stop there. When you get the chance, throw apparently innocent questions their way that highlight the contradiction between their words and actions. You might say something like: "Hey, do you still think punctuality is as important as you used to say?" And if you really want to seal the deal, casually mention past situations that contrast with their current behavior. Something like: "I remember when you used to get so upset about others being late. It's interesting to see how perspectives change over time, isn't it?"

With this technique, you're basically reflecting and amplifying the person's hypocritical behavior, taking it to the extreme in an obvious way using their own example. The goal is to make the hypocrite face their own contradictions in a way they can't simply ignore or dismiss.

Of course, this technique requires patience and subtlety. It's not about openly mocking the hypocrite or making dramatic scenes. It's about being consistent, strategic, and a bit theatrical in your approach. And who knows, maybe seeing themselves reflected this way, the hypocrite might begin to question themselves and make some real changes.

But let's be realistic, not all hypocrites will have an epiphany and transform overnight. Some are so caught up in their own narrative that not even the clearest mirror will make them change. In these cases, you might have to accept that some people simply aren't willing or able to face their own contradictions. And that's when you have to decide how much energy you're willing to invest in someone who doesn't want to change.

Another effective strategy for confronting hypocrites is to point out their hypocrisy directly, but tactfully. This involves "painting their actions red" through concrete facts, acknowledging that we all suffer from cognitive dissonance[9] to some degree and that the "funnel law"[10]—bad for others, good for oneself—is a common human tendency. However, pointing out hypocrisy carries a paradox: it tends to be more effective when done in private than in public. In

---

[9] Psychological theory introduced by Leon Festinger (1957). Describes mental discomfort when holding contradictory beliefs. Studies show people will often change memories rather than core beliefs to reduce this tension.

[10] Psychological principle similar to Fundamental Attribution Error. Research shows people attribute their own mistakes to circumstances but others' mistakes to character flaws. Present across all cultures but varies in intensity

private conversations, it can even be useful to warn that if such hypocrisy persists, it might be exposed publicly in the future. This tactic often motivates the hypocrite to reconsider their actions or change their behavior. By addressing hypocrisy this way, we not only face the problem directly but also offer an opportunity for growth and reflection, both for the hypocrite and for ourselves.

Give them one chance, not two.

The Moochers' Bazaar

You might know them as opportunists, freeloaders, parasites, users, or advantage-takers. They're the ones who, without hesitation, seek to extract maximum benefit from others' generosity and good nature. They're the type of people to whom you give an inch, and they not only take a mile but make themselves comfortable and demand even more.

Sound familiar? Of course it does. It's that "friend" who always needs rides everywhere but mysteriously never contributes to gas money. Or that coworker who dumps their tasks on you as if they were your boss. Or worse still, the relative who shows up at your house unannounced, treating it like an all-inclusive hotel.

These moochers are experts at living like royalty at others' expense, and the worst part is they're not even ashamed. On the contrary, they strut around proud of their "cleverness," as if being an opportunist were a university degree. Most irritating is that these specimens are masters of social camouflage. They're charismatic, make you feel important, and before you know it, they're squeezing you like an orange for juice.

To identify these moochers, notice how they're always available to receive but rarely to give, they have a PhD in turning THEIR problems into YOUR problems, and they avoid any situation that requires effort or commitment on their part. Their favorite phrase might be "Can you do me a favor?" - and believe me, what they're going to ask for will never be small - likewise, you'll never hear from them "How can I help you?"

We won't revisit setting boundaries as that's already clear; sometimes dealing with these people requires more creative approaches. One advantage of moochers is that they often pride themselves on their behavior, even hiding it behind innocent phrases like "Well, if you don't ask, you don't get" - implying they have nothing to lose by asking for the moon and hoping you're too nice to refuse. And this is an advantage because these people can be handled better with humor and sarcasm than with sincerity and disgust. For example, when they ask for the moon and stars, you can reply "And what else would you like with that? A coffee and cookies? Anything else?"

If you're tired of these shameless opportunists constantly trying to take advantage of your generosity, here are some unconventional strategies to deal with them:

1. The Surprise Contract

Next time they ask for an extreme favor, pull out a "contract" prepared in advance - or start drafting one on the spot, with a napkin and pen, with a big CONTRACT title. Include absurd clauses like "In return, the beneficiary must sing the national anthem naked in public." The ridiculousness of the situation will make them realize they're asking for something beyond possible. In the appendices, I've included a perfect contract for these purposes.

2. The Impossible Favor

When they ask for something, respond with exaggerated enthusiasm and offer to do much more than requested. "Of course! And what else would you like? Want me to lend you money? Sure! I'll sell my house, move my family to a tent, and give you all my savings. When do we start?" Do it in a comic tone, not sarcastic: you're mocking the request, don't make it seem like you're offended. This false and mocking excessive willingness will make them back off quickly.

3. The Uncomfortable Interrogation Technique

Bombard the moocher with uncomfortable and detailed questions every time they ask for something: "Why do you need this? Why me? Don't you have other friends? Do you do this often? Do you owe similar favors to anyone else? Have you finished paying your debt to them?" Don't stop pressing until they uncomfortably retract their selfish request.

As mentioned in the first point, in the appendices you'll find a fiendishly complicated contract that's almost impossible to read, let alone fulfill - due to its fine print and the obligations the signer takes on with you. Consider making a copy and carrying it with you for when any of these moochers asks you for something. When they do, ask what they'd give in exchange for your blessing, tell them you have a "little contract" you'd like them to sign and not to worry about the fine print as it's just a formality. It's a touch of dark humor that will make your position clear. And if they dare to sign it, keep it and respond that now all that's left is to "validate the signer's information," as if it were some bureaucratic process to complete, and leave it at that.

If after your joke they insist - because they surely will - and say "Okay, but seriously: are you going to tell me/help me/lend me... such thing?" Your answer will simply be "NO" with an exaggerated head shake from side to side. The previous joking response has already smoothed the situation and the message has been made clear.

There are people who, after all your effort to achieve something, expect you to share your experience, formulas, and learnings of months and years in a ten-minute conversation. I'm not talking about those who want to be entertained by your odysseys, but those who seriously want to obtain the same as you in exchange for buying you a miserable coffee. For them, you've already gone through the tears and blood, and they feel entitled to all your know-how.

Don't feel guilty about responding negatively to their request. Remember that the formula for success consists of just two things: First, "Never tell everything you know." And the second? Read the first one again...

Asking Without Shame

After unmasking the moochers, there's something we can learn from them: these characters, as irritating as they are, have something to teach us. No, it's not about becoming unscrupulous opportunists, but about adopting an attitude that many of us, in our effort to be "good people," have forgotten: asking without shame.

Think about it, how many opportunities have you let slip by because you didn't dare ask for something? Maybe it was that raise you deserved or that date with someone you liked. Moochers, in their brazenness, have perfected something many of us struggle with: clearly expressing what they want without feeling guilty about it.

The shame of asking is like a mental parasite that feeds on your potential. It whispers in your ear that something isn't for you, that you're bothering others, that you should settle. The battle is lost before it begins. How can we send this limiting shame flying? There are several techniques:

When it's something important or that you've been thinking about and turning over in your mind, consider mental rehearsal. Visualize yourself asking for what you want with confidence. Imagine different scenarios and responses, mentally preparing yourself for any outcome. It's like doing mental push-ups before entering the ring. But always carry with you the understanding that these dialogues, no matter how much you practice, will NEVER go exactly as planned. In this sense, I'll share a lesson from my years as a speaker: don't focus on memorizing the words you want to say but, rather, work on a dialogue structure you can move within depending on the responses you can imagine.

Second, the 5-second rule. This is for those "train is coming: are you going to hop on or let it pass?" moments. When you feel the impulse to ask for something, count to 5 and do it. Don't give your brain time to sabotage you with doubts. Remember that no dialogue will turn out exactly as you expected. This is like ripping off a band-aid from a wound, quick and without thinking too much. If things don't go as expected, well, at least you tried! It's behind you, next!

As a third technique for intermediate points, there's the hypothetical "NO." Ask yourself: "What's the worst that can happen if they say no?" Generally, the answer is less catastrophic than you imagine. Unless you're proposing marriage to someone in public and they say no, in which case, good luck with that.

And finally, the value focus. When asking for something, concentrate on the value you bring or how your request could benefit the other person. This way, you won't feel like you're begging, but offering something of value. In this sense, have you noticed how some people begin their requests with "I need such and such"? For them, it's as if the world was eagerly waiting to satisfy their needs. Well, let me tell you something: people don't care what you and I need. Yes, that's harsh. You need a favor? Too bad, but that's not others' problem. This is where you need to offer value. So, how do you ask without sounding like a demanding egocentric? Try something more subtle. Instead of dropping an "I need," try "I'm looking for" or "I've been interested in..." And if you want to go a step further, try finding common ground before launching your request. Something like "I know you've also been looking for something similar" or "I remember you mentioned something about this before." This way, you're not asking out of nowhere, but building on a foundation of mutual understanding. The key is to ask with tact, not with demands.

Of course, it's not about becoming a shameless person who asks without consideration. The key is finding that assertiveness that allows you to express desires clearly and directly, but without crossing the line. And here's where the part that differentiates us from moochers comes in: understanding and respecting that the other person has EVERY RIGHT to tell us NO. This understanding is liberating. It allows you to ask without the pressure of always getting a yes, and prepares you to handle rejection with maturity. Because sometimes, even if you ask with all the confidence in the world, the answer will be no. And that's perfectly fine.

So the next time you feel that knot in your stomach before asking for something, think about the moochers. Not to imitate their lack of consideration, but to remember that asking is a right, not a privilege. And who knows, you might be surprised at how many doors open when you dare to knock.

Nothing Is As Important As It Seems

Forced kindness is like a ridiculous mask you put on every morning, one that squeezes and makes you feel trapped, woven from threads of others' expectations and dyed in the color of "what will people say." You wake up thinking about how you should act, which smiles to fake, which elaborate words to throw out, everything measured with the precision of an obsessive surgeon.

How many times have you nodded politely in a meeting while inside you wanted to tell it all to go to hell? How many times have you sent messages full of smiling emojis to people you don't even care about? The reality is that we live in an endless theater, where everyone plays the role of the "pleasant person," as if our existence depended on it.

But here comes the uncomfortable truth: nobody cares as much as you think. Everyone is so wrapped up in their own bubble of worries, desires, and personal dramas that they barely have time to notice your gestures or analyze your words. While you're killing yourself trying to appear kind, they're thinking about their next meeting, the fight they had this morning, or what they'll eat tonight.

It's as if we were in a city full of floating bubbles, each with a person absorbed in their own world. We cross paths, bump into each other, but rarely truly penetrate another's bubble. And yet, how much energy we waste trying to manipulate how we're perceived by those who barely pay attention to us!

Genuine kindness is a valuable gift, a sincere expression of human connection. But forced kindness is a prison you put yourself in, an unnecessary waste of your vital energy. It's like trying to control the weather: you can worry all you want about whether it will rain tomorrow, but your worries won't change a single drop.

Freeing yourself from this compulsive need to please doesn't mean becoming rude or insensitive. Rather, it means finding a balance between the basic respect we all deserve and the authenticity you owe yourself. It means understanding that you can't control what others think of you, and trying to do so is as futile as trying to catch the wind with your hands.

The next time you find yourself forcing a smile or writing an excessively cordial message, ask yourself: Is this really necessary? Am I being kind out of genuine consideration for the other person, or am I acting out of fear of being judged? The answer might surprise you and, more importantly, might free you.

Nothing is as important as we think. Not the opinions of others, not social appearances, not the judgments we fear. True freedom begins when we understand that most of the things we worry about are like passing clouds in an infinite sky: apparently solid, but fundamentally empty.

Don't Take Anything at Face Value

We live in an age of willful ignorance, an era of swallowing everything whole, and without a bit of critical thinking, we're at the mercy of a world full of falsehoods and nonsense. Make no mistake, this isn't just about questioning things because it sounds good—critical thinking is that almost forgotten skill that will help us stop believing in pipe dreams and false promises.

Sometimes appealing to critical thinking can be seen as a lack of kindness, which is why I've decided to dedicate a section to this topic in these pages, although critical thinking will be a subject I'll explore in a future publication. First: do yourself a favor and stop believing every story you're told. People spout nonsense they've never questioned, and many repeat it as if they were sacred words. In the world of TikTok, everyone swallows everything whole. Don't be one of them. If something sounds so incredible that it makes you feel like "anything is possible," there's almost certainly a catch. From politicians and "spiritual gurus" to ridiculous offers on social media, everyone has their price and agenda. Learn to spot the hook.

"Blind faith" is the direct path to stupidity. And don't confuse this with bitterness or cynicism—this is mere survival intelligence. People who tell you to "believe without questioning" are usually selling you smoke. Whether it's a story, a cause, or a magic supplement, everything usually comes loaded with fiction, or at least some bias.

Being critical isn't the same as being a professional contrarian. Keep an open mind, sure, but not so open that your brain falls out. Gather data, analyze, and use common sense, even though these days it seems to be the least common of senses. Reality is complex, and truth rarely shows itself in simple or comfortable ways. Developing selective reading habits is key: but it's not about reading for reading's sake—it's about selecting reliable and varied sources. Don't lock yourself into a single perspective. Read opposing opinions, research authors' backgrounds, and verify information with multiple sources. Critical reading will help you identify biases and weak arguments.

Get used to uncomfortable questions—they're the exercise that strengthens your mind. If something challenges you, don't run away; face it and examine whether your beliefs have any value or if they're just castles in the sand. Changing your mind isn't betrayal—it's growth. Fools are those who cling to their opinions as if they were the only thing keeping them alive. Moreover, practicing active listening will help you truly understand what's being said. Pay attention to details, detect inconsistencies, and ask clarifying questions.

The next time you face a claim you distrust, use the Socratic method[11]: ask yourself what evidence supports it, what's the source, if there are alternatives, and what assumptions are being made. This method forces you to dig deeper beneath the surface and not accept anything without rigorous evaluation. Recognize and control your biases—we all have cognitive biases that cloud our judgment. Identify yours, like confirmation bias or the halo effect[12], and be aware of how your experiences and beliefs influence your perception of reality. Ask yourself: Why do I think this way? Am I being objective?

Don't settle for the first answer you're given to any question you have. Explore different approaches and perspectives to solve problems. Don't accept something as truth just because an authority figure says it. Research on your own and form your own opinion. Practice informed decision-making: before deciding something important, gather all relevant information, evaluate available options, and consider both short and long-term consequences. Don't rush—critical thinking values quality over speed.

---

[11] Ancient Greek teaching method developed by Socrates (470-399 BCE). Uses probing questions to expose assumptions and clarify thinking. Modern studies show it improves critical thinking skills by 66% compared to traditional instruction.

[12] Cognitive bias discovered by Thorndike (1920). One positive trait influences overall evaluation. Studies show attractive people receive 20% higher performance ratings despite equal performance.

Furthermore, surround yourself with critical minds. The people around you influence your way of thinking. Seek the company of individuals who value critical thinking, who challenge your ideas constructively, and who inspire you to be better.

Critical thinking is a wonderful shield against manipulation. Advertising, news, social media... they all have an agenda, and your duty is to identify what it is before buying into their story. Don't feel immune to manipulation. No one is. But if you train yourself to question and think for yourself, you become a much harder target.

Thinking critically isn't about being negative or "the Grinch of logic." It's about seeing things with a complete perspective and making well-founded decisions, as if you were the only one responsible for what enters your head. So, the next time someone asks you to believe in something "because it's always been that way" or "because everyone believes it," wake up and question it. Investigate, inform yourself, and consider your options. And if the evidence points in another direction, dare to change your mind!

Epilogue: A Postscript to the Golden Rule

As we finish this journey, it's crucial to reiterate that stopping being excessively nice doesn't mean swinging to the other extreme and disregarding others' feelings or needs. The goal is to find a middle ground: knowing how to defend your own interests without trampling on others' rights.

One of the biggest misunderstandings about assertiveness is confusing it with selfishness or aggressiveness. Nothing could be further from the truth. Assertiveness is establishing boundaries, knowing where your rights end and others' begin. It allows you to respect your own needs and recognize others' without carrying guilt. Being assertive doesn't mean running over anyone; it means ensuring your rights aren't ignored.

In these times, it's easy to mistake a smile or casual conversation for real friendship. But true friendship transcends courtesy and sporadic favors. This doesn't mean everyone's trying to manipulate us, but that authentic relationships are defined beyond simple kindness. Understanding this allows us to set boundaries without feeling guilty for not always being available or accommodating.

Another point is the social media validation trap. Many forget that a virtual thumbs up has no relevance to self-worth or relationships. Self-esteem should come from within, not from a superficial online gesture. It's vital to avoid these meta-indicators of approval that only distract us from real connections and sense of identity.

Silence is an underestimated tool for self-assertion. Sometimes, the absence of words is the most powerful statement, conveying security and control when speaking would only cause conflicts or weaken your position. Silence can set a boundary by itself, implicitly indicating that not everything deserves a response.

With clear boundaries and without depending on superficial validation, you find a balance between self-respect and empathy. Assertiveness isn't about being rigid without reason, but about being true to yourself and acting with confidence while also recognizing others' humanity.

We've all heard the Golden Rule: that "universal jewel" that sounds so profound but sometimes proves quite useless. Everyone repeats it like parrots, carries it tattooed on their tongue as if saying it meant understanding it. But understanding it, truly understanding it... that's another story.

The Golden Rule comes in two versions, like medicine: the "pretty" version and the "antiseptic" one. The first says: "Treat others as you would like to be treated." Nice, profound, but completely misinterpreted. The second is for the cautious: "Don't do to others what you wouldn't want done to you." This is the defensive edition, but at least it keeps your hands clean and conscience intact.

Now, don't fool yourself – it doesn't end there. Both versions of this rule come with hidden clauses, uncomfortable postscripts that nobody mentions, but which are what really matter.

The first postscript says: "Only you decide how much you can take." Because being a good person is one thing, and being everyone's emotional garbage dump is another. You don't have to carry others' misery just because, much less play hero in problems you neither sought nor understand. Not all battles are yours, so choose wisely.

And then there's the Postscript to the Postscript, a second clause nobody will tell you: "You don't have to deal with anyone's crap." Being a good person isn't synonymous with being everyone's doormat. Let everyone carry their own ghosts and learn to deal with their decisions. You, meanwhile, focus on your own business.

Curiously, these two additions are what truly matter, but literature never mentions them. Perhaps because both adjustments don't sound spiritual enough, or because saying "crap" isn't very zen-like. But the truth is that these are the pieces of advice that really work in real life, the ones that let you keep your dignity intact while navigating this sea of others' expectations.

Appendix 1: A Course in Sarcasm

Have you noticed that some people seem to have a superpower for responding intelligently to any silly comment that comes their way? Yes, those masters of wit who can disarm an uncomfortable question with a surgeon's precision and the grace of a clown on fire. While you're still scratching your head at the impertinence, they've already delivered a response so sharp that even the original questioner starts questioning their own existence.

Not all of us are born with the ability to give witty comebacks instantly, that spark that turns a terrible situation into a lesson in "don't mess where you don't belong." But what if I told you that you could train this incredible skill? What if there was a "manual of intelligent responses" for all those stupid questions people throw at you when they're trying to criticize, mock, or simply mess up your life?

Well, that's exactly what you have here in this appendix: a collection of 50 passive-aggressive questions we've all faced at some point, along with responses specifically designed to set boundaries without wasting time on unnecessary explanations. Each question comes with its context and a response that blends wit, assertiveness, and just the right touch of sarcasm that says "this is where you stop."

But isn't sarcasm bad? It depends. The kind we're dealing with here has a purpose; it's just another tool in your authenticity arsenal. You're not obligated to memorize every response or become the king of biting wit. Take what serves you, adapt the responses to your style, and above all, remember that the goal isn't to hurt, but to set clear boundaries with attitude.

Great! Here are the first 10 Q&As with their explanations:

1. "How's that weight/baldness/(any physical trait) going?"

R/ "Perfect as always."

This type of comment aims to embarrass or make someone feel bad by negatively highlighting a physical trait. The response conveys confidence and dodges the attack with a dose of self-assurance that doesn't allow for debate. By defining yourself as "perfect," you make it clear there's nothing to change or question, disarming the criticism without engaging in confrontation.

---

2. "And why do you like/did you do/choose that?"

R/ "Because I can."

Here, personal choices are questioned with the intention of casting doubt on or criticizing tastes or decisions. The brief and decisive response suggests you don't need to explain or justify your choices. The firmness blocks discussion and places a barrier against attempts to question your autonomy.

---

3. "And what's that for?"

R/ "For you to wonder."

This question disdainfully judges personal preferences or tastes, implying they lack value or utility. The ironic twist in the response returns the burden of the question to the asker, showing it's unnecessary. Additionally, it shows you have no interest in justifying your motives because there's no need to explain them to anyone.

---

4. "Aren't you ashamed/embarrassed?"

R/ "Should I be?"

Judging an action or decision seeking to generate guilt or discomfort is the aim of this question. Responding with another question that makes the speaker doubt their own values creates an uncomfortable pause. This rhetorical counter-strike invites questioning the relevance of feeling shame for something that's clearly not shameful to you.

5. "Why don't you try it another way?"

R/ "If I wanted to, I would have already."

The implicit suggestion here is that the current method is inadequate, questioning capabilities or judgment. The response makes it clear that your choice is intentional and needs no correction. By saying you would have changed if you wanted to, you convey authority over your decisions and close the door to unsolicited suggestions.

6. "Do you really think that will work?"

R/ "I hope so. We'll see."

Sowing doubts about the viability of an idea or action is an attempt to discourage or discredit. With a firm and neutral tone, this response avoids falling into the doubt the speaker tries to instill, while not revealing insecurity. You make it clear you're aware of the possible outcome and, at the same time, don't give them the satisfaction of questioning yourself.

7. "Don't you think you could do better?"

R/ "Sure, but I like seeing it this way from down here."

The response discredits the indirect criticism implying insufficient effort, showing that the person isn't fazed by the supposed "improvement" they could achieve. It makes clear that external criticism doesn't move their standard or effort.

---

8. "What made you think that?"

R/ "Your inspiration, I suppose."

Questioning intelligence or judgment seeks to destabilize. This response redirects the question back with a tone that subtly suggests the other person might not understand the decision, and could even be the reason for the "error." Thus, it maintains control by not justifying at all.

---

9. "Are you sure that's the best option?"

R/ "Without doubt. And I can tell by the look on your face."

Doubt about a choice seeks to generate insecurity. But the response not only affirms certainty in the decision but also turns the other person's doubt into an ironic "validation." It provides unshakeable confidence and makes the other person appear more insecure.

---

10. "Aren't you worried about how this might affect things?"

R/ "Sure, but that's what makes it fun!"

Here, they try to make you feel guilty by implying potential negative consequences. But the response breaks through any guilt by responding with a touch of defiant nonchalance. It shows a confident attitude, willing to face consequences without wasting time on doubts.

Here are questions 11-20 with their explanations:

11. "Why don't you follow what everyone else does?"

R/ "I enjoy missing out on the classics."

The pressure to conform and follow the majority is clear in this question. The response indicates that what "everyone" follows isn't of interest, as if asking was more boring than any "norm." It emphasizes independence and shows that going against the grain is something to be enjoyed, not suffered.

---

12. "Don't you think that's a bit excessive?"

R/ "Modesty isn't really my strong suit."

Labeling something as "excessive" seeks to generate doubt or shame. But the response in an almost proud tone suggests that this intensity is not only intentional but characteristic. It frames the action as a personal trademark that needs no permission or excuses.

---

13. "How did you reach that conclusion?"

R/ "Using the same method you used to ask."

Questioning the thought process is a way of attacking intelligence. The response turns the doubt back in the same tone, suggesting the other person has no authority over reasoning. It maintains mystery and avoids any attempt to invade mental processes.

---

14. "Why do you insist on doing it this way?"

R/ "Because repetition works. Just look at us."

Criticizing perseverance in a method is an attempt to discredit. The response takes up repetition as an ironic concept, implying that the other person also repeats their questions, perhaps unsuccessfully. It suggests that if anyone should reconsider something, it's not the one responding.

15. "What if it doesn't turn out as you expect?"

R/ "Then it'll turn out as you expected."

Doubt about success seeks to generate insecurity about the action. But the response suggests that, regardless of the outcome, the person is already prepared. It implies that the risk and success are theirs, but if it fails, it wouldn't be any surprise. The criticism loses effect when the other person seems unshakeable in the face of failure.

16. "Why don't you look for another alternative?"

R/ "This one just looks too entertaining."

Suggesting other options implies the current one is insufficient. But the response indicates having control over the choice, and that other options were discarded by preference, not lack of judgment. It highlights that the choice is intentional, not the result of poor process.

17. "Don't you think it's a bit complicated?"

R/ "Yes, but it's a type of fun few understand."

Labeling something as "complicated" suggests it's unnecessarily difficult. But the response removes all negative connotation from complexity, presenting it as something exclusive and therefore more valuable. By acknowledging that "few understand," it turns the criticism into a validation of one's own capability and taste for challenges.

---

18. "Why don't you try something different?"

R/ "Why should I, when this already works?"

Criticizing lack of variety or flexibility is the objective here. But the response disarms the criticism by implying that the questioner lacks practical vision. By emphasizing functionality, it reinforces the value of the current decision and makes clear that change for change's sake isn't necessarily progress.

---

19. "How do you justify that decision?"

R/ "With the same data you ignored."

Questioning the morality or logic of a choice seeks to destabilize. But here it implies that the questioner is uninformed, which returns the criticism with precision. The implication that they overlooked something puts them on the defensive and prevents the questioning from continuing.

---

20. "Why don't you prioritize differently?"

R/ "Because this way already gives me results."

This question implies poor priority management. But the response minimizes the "suggestion" and reaffirms that results validate the current choice, making clear that any change would be unnecessary. It's an elegant way of saying "my priorities are better than you think."

Here are questions 21-30 with their explanations:

21. "What's stopping you from improving?"

R/ "The same thing that's stopping you from understanding."

Criticizing a supposed lack of progress or effort is the purpose here. Answering this way puts the lack of improvement and the questioner's lack of understanding on the same level, suggesting they might not be in a position to offer advice. The response shows that the supposed "stagnation" is a mistaken perception.

---

22. "Why don't you consider the possible drawbacks?"

R/ "Because I prefer results."

Suggesting negligence in planning is this question's objective. But the response addresses the criticism without justifying anything, shifting focus to the value of concrete achievements. The implication is that while the questioner focuses on problems, you focus on producing results.

———————————

23. "Why don't you adapt to changes?"

R/ "Because I adapt to what matters."

Criticizing resistance to change seeks to destabilize. But here, the focus is on selectivity, implying that only significant changes deserve attention. It suggests that the questioner changes without clear reason, while you have defined criteria.

———————————

24. "Don't you feel overwhelmed?"

R/ "Curious that you do."

Implying inability to handle responsibilities is a clear attack. This response redirects the discomfort back to the questioner, suggesting the problem might lie in their perception or their own handling of things. It reinforces the idea that you're in control.

---

25. "Why hadn't you thought of this before?"

R/ "Because I was busy doing it first."

Criticizing lack of foresight or intelligence is the objective here. But the response emphasizes that execution is more valuable than mere planning. It's a reminder that thinking isn't enough if it doesn't translate into results, implying that the questioner gives too much importance to theory.

---

26. "Why don't you focus on what's essential?"

R/ "Because some details matter too."

This question suggests scattered focus or lack of concentration. But the response returns the criticism by highlighting the importance of nuances, suggesting that the questioner only sees part of the picture. It's a subtle way of reminding them that complexity also has value.

---

27. "Why don't you set better priorities?"

R/ "Because this way I don't miss anything."

Implying poor time or resource management is the purpose of this question. But the response suggests that the questioner doesn't understand the difference between prioritizing and discarding. Highlighting that "nothing is missed" implies having an effective organization that others simply can't see.

---

28. "What do you hope to achieve with that?"

R/ "Enough for you to notice."

Questioning the effectiveness or purpose of an action seeks to destabilize. But this response is effective because it turns the question into evidence of your achievements' success or visibility. It emphasizes that you're already making an impact, which minimizes the questioner's doubt.

---

29. "Why don't you simplify things?"

R/ "Because this is the only way to do it right."

Criticizing unnecessary complication is the objective here. But this is a subtle reminder that complexity is necessary when aiming for excellence. The response implies that whoever asks for simplification probably doesn't understand the need for detail in quality situations.

30. "What's preventing you from moving forward?"

R/ "Nothing you'd notice."

Implying stagnation or lack of initiative is a clear attack. But this response evades the criticism with a declaration of independence and confidence, implying that any "obstacle" is too subtle for others to perceive.

Here are questions 31-40 with their explanations:

31. "Why don't you join the others?"

R/ "Why follow them?"

This question criticizes exclusion or lack of participation. The response turns the question back, inviting reflection on whether blindly following "others" is as valuable as they assume. It deflects attention and suggests that being oneself is superior to "joining in."

32. "Why don't you do something productive?"

R/ "This seems as productive as your questions."

Implying idleness or lack of value is this questioning's objective. Here sarcasm is key. It responds as if their question were an example of "unproductivity," making clear that the criticism is empty and misdirected.

---

33. "Why don't you exercise more?"

R/ "At my pace, I don't need to."

Commenting on health habits in an implicitly critical way seeks to shame. But the response is almost dismissive: no "extra" effort is needed because they're already satisfied with themselves. It highlights their positive self-perception without need for additional effort, contradicting the question's judgment.

---

34. "Why are you still living with your parents?"

R/ "I get along with them, do you?"

Criticizing personal independence or maturity is the clear objective here. But the response redirects the question to the asker's family relationships, disarming the criticism about independence. It leaves their possible discomfort hanging in the air without revealing or justifying one's own situation.

---

35. "Why do you always choose the easy way?"

R/ "Because I make it work."

The implication of lack of effort or ambition is clear in this question. But the response reinterprets "easy" as something intentional and effective. It implies that choosing the easy way is pragmatic, highlighting the responder's skill and control versus supposed "comfort."

---

36. "Why don't you try something more interesting?"

R/ "Define interesting."

Criticizing lack of creativity or enthusiasm is the objective here. But asking them to define "interesting" throws back the responsibility for that subjective criticism, forcing the other to reflect and breaking down the implicit accusation.

---

37. "Why don't you take a break from all that work?"

R/ "Because I rest better without your advice."

The implicit suggestion of overwork or lack of balance seeks to destabilize. But this response suggests that the unsolicited advice is intrusive and that rest, balance, or personal health are well managed. It maintains a dismissive self-confidence toward the "concerned" opinion-giver.

38. "Why don't you look for a better job?"

R/ "Because this one is perfect for me."

Criticizing current job satisfaction is an attempt to generate doubt. But this response reinforces the idea that the current job is exactly what the person wants. It suggests a sense of complete satisfaction, making the interlocutor understand that commenting on it is unnecessary and futile.

39. "Why don't you try something more challenging?"

R/ "Why should I, when this is more than enough?"

The implication of excessive comfort or lack of ambition is clear here. But the response is from someone who finds their current activity already sufficient. It conveys calm superiority, making the question seem like a comment from someone who underestimates without reason.

40. "Why don't you get more involved in the community?"

R/ "I prefer to observe from a distance."

Criticizing lack of social participation is this question's objective. But the response reflects a deliberate personal choice and shows the individual's independence in maintaining distance, suggesting that involvement isn't necessary for someone of their caliber.

Here are questions 41-50 with their explanations:

41. "Why don't you try being more positive?"

R/ "I prefer being realistic."

Implying negativity or pessimism seeks to emotionally destabilize. But this response redefines "negativity" as realism, disarming the emotional argument and suggesting that the questioner confuses optimism with superficiality.

---

42. "Why are you always so negative?"

R/ "Why don't you try a different approach?"

Directly criticizing someone's attitude is a clear attack. But the response leaves "negativity" as a matter of perception and suggests that if there's discomfort, it's the other person's issue. It returns the "problem" to its source, shifting attention from the criticized to the critic.

43. "Why don't you join a group or club?"

R/ "I don't see the need to fill space."

This question criticizes isolation or lack of socialization. But the response deactivates the assumption that socializing in groups is a necessity or achievement. By implying that joining a group is just "filling space," it suggests they don't need company to validate their worth, projecting independence.

44. "Why don't you try to be more efficient?"

R/ "Because I already do too much."

Implying inefficiency or lack of productivity is the clear objective here. But the response is decisive: it makes clear that their contribution is already significant and that any suggestion to "improve" is irrelevant. With a single phrase, it discredits the insinuation and marks the other's perception as incorrect.

45. "Don't you think you're wasting your time?"

R/ "Oh, do you have too much of yours?"

Judging personal time use is a form of attack. But instead of defending, this response returns pressure to the questioner, questioning their authority to evaluate others' time. By shifting focus to the other person's time, it suggests the question is intrusive.

---

46. "Why don't you do something useful with your life?"

R/ "Because I'm enjoying it."

Criticizing the direction or purpose of someone's life is a very personal judgment. With this response, the idea of "usefulness" is redefined. "Enjoying" becomes the central purpose, avoiding any need for justification or external validation about how one lives.

---

47. "Don't you think you're too distracted?"

R/ "Only when listening to unimportant things."

Implying lack of attention or responsibility is a form of attack. But this response restructures supposed "distraction" into a selective act: lack of attention isn't a defect but a choice regarding what they consider irrelevant. By questioning the importance of what's being said, it implies their attention is well-directed.

---

48. "Why don't you stop procrastinating?"

R/ "Even for that, I have a plan."

Criticizing lack of productivity is the clear objective here. But the response takes the term "procrastinating" and gives it an unexpected twist, showing that everything, even breaks, follows a personal structure. By referring to procrastination as a "plan," it neutralizes any criticism.

---

49. "Don't you think you lack maturity?"

R/ "Thanks, I'll take that as a compliment."

Judging someone's level of maturity is a direct attack. But instead of taking offense or justifying, the response adopts the criticism as a compliment, removing power from any suggestion of "immaturity" and returning the comment with elegance. This twist disarms the question and shows that the respondent doesn't feel the urgency to meet others' expectations.

---

50. "Why are you always making things complicated?"

R/ "It's how I keep myself entertained."

Criticizing the tendency to create unnecessary complications is this question's objective. But the response turns the criticism into a creativity exercise: complicating things is simply a way to avoid boredom. By taking control of the situation and defining their own approach as entertaining, it shows they don't need to simplify anything to meet external expectations.

This concludes the full set of 50 sarcastic responses. Would you like any clarification or adjustment to any of them?

Appendix 2: 19 Missions to Stop Being Too Nice

Now it's time to put yourself to the test. Theory is beautiful, but it's in practice where you really start to see results. That's why I've included this collection of 19 missions that will help you deprogram that compulsive need to please everyone and show you, tangibly, that the world doesn't end when you stop being their eternal people-pleaser.

Why do I call them missions? Because each of these exercises is a small covert operation against your mental programming of extreme "niceness." They are practical exercises that will take you out of your comfort zone and make you question those behavioral patterns you've been clinging to as if they were sacred commandments.

There's no specific order for completing these missions. You can start with the one that seems least threatening or dive straight into the one that makes you most uncomfortable—after all, breaking the mold has never been comfortable. What's important is that after each mission, you take a moment to reflect on the experience. Was it as terrible as you imagined? Did the world end? Is there no reason to live? Is guilt really such a horrible thing, or are you exaggerating it? Did anyone die because you weren't "nice"?

Moreover, sit down and analyze: How difficult was it really? How did people react? And most importantly: did anything fundamental change in your life or relationships? I bet you'll discover that the universe kept moving, that the Earth didn't stop spinning, and that being authentic, although uncomfortable at first, is much more liberating than you thought.

These missions are a complete laboratory for authenticity. They're your opportunity to prove, firsthand, that you don't need others' constant approval to exist, that setting boundaries doesn't make you a bad person, and that true freedom begins when you stop living to please others.

Ready to start? Choose your first mission and prepare to discover that being less nice and more authentic isn't just possible—it's tremendously liberating.

The Missions

MISSION 1: Today, you won't shower. Go to work without showering or shaving. Don't explicitly tell anyone you haven't groomed yourself, but for 24 hours, you won't shower.

MISSION 2: Today you're going to pretend to be deaf on two occasions. That is, you're going to deliberately act as if you haven't heard something.

Someone will say something to you, and you won't respond, look, or turn around—nothing. Observe your own silence and control that impulse to be polite. When they try to get your attention again, don't say "sorry" or justify that you didn't hear; just turn and say "Yes?" so they'll repeat what you ignored.

MISSION 3: Today, you won't initiate any conversations; let everything come to you naturally. Don't try to fill any silence, and if you need something, don't ask for it—state it. For example: Instead of saying "Where are the reports for...?" say "I need the reports for..." If someone asks if something's wrong, always say "Not at all."

MISSION 4: This is a mission you must spread over several days. You need to achieve 5 refusals to requests without explanations over consecutive days. If you said "NO" twice in one day, add two points; if the next day you gave three refusals, add three more points, and you've reached 5 points. But if you go a day without any refusals, you must start over from 0. Remember, only "NOs" to requests count.

MISSION 5: Today you're going to eat something you'd normally avoid for fear of what others might think. Order that greasy burger, that caloric dessert, or that exotic dish. Eat with gusto, without excuses or explanations. If someone comments, simply say "I was craving it" and continue enjoying.

MISSION 6: At some point during the day, express an unpopular opinion. It doesn't have to be offensive, just something most people wouldn't agree with. Stand firm in your position; don't yield to the pressure to please or retract. If questioned, calmly say "That's my opinion, you don't have to like it."

MISSION 7: Today, when someone asks for help with a task, you'll say "I can't" without offering any explanation. It doesn't matter if you have time or not, simply say "I can't" and observe how they react. Resist the urge to justify yourself or give in to any pressure. The answer is "I can't" and that's it. This mission doesn't count toward Mission 4's score.

MISSION 8: This mission will only be completed when you willingly let someone make a mistake. It's not about inducing error; it's about letting them do what they want to do, even knowing it will go wrong. If you see a colleague making a mistake or a friend about to make a bad decision, resist the urge to intervene or correct. Watch how the situation unfolds without getting involved. Remember, everyone is responsible for their own actions.

MISSION 9: Today, in at least one interaction, you're going to speak deliberately slower than normal. Take your time to respond, pause between phrases. If you notice impatience in your listener, don't speed up.

Maintain your rhythm, own your words and your tempo.

MISSION 10: Today, you're going to point out an obvious problem that everyone avoids mentioning. Be direct and firm, without beating around the bush.

MISSION 11: Today, you're going to maintain eye contact during all your conversations. In fact, you're going to try to remember the eye color of at least five of your conversation partners. Don't look away out of shyness or discomfort. Maintain a firm and friendly gaze, even if the topic gets intense. Your gaze communicates security and engagement in the interaction.

MISSION 12: Today, you're going to sit in the front seat in any situation involving seats (a class, conference, public transport, etc.). Don't hide in the back. Claim your space and your presence. If you feel people looking, remember: you're exactly where you should be.

MISSION 13: Today, you're going to start a conversation with a complete stranger. It could be in the supermarket line, in the elevator, or anywhere else. Make a casual comment or give a sincere compliment. The goal isn't to forge a deep friendship, but to practice initiating interactions without fear of rejection.

MISSION 14: Today, on at least one occasion, you're going to say "I don't understand" when someone explains something to you. Don't pretend to understand out of fear of appearing foolish. Ask for clarification without apologizing, even if you've understood completely. After the explanation, even if you've understood and it's clear to everyone, say "I still don't understand." If they throw it back at you asking "What exactly don't you understand?" repeat "I want absolute clarity about the whole matter." It doesn't matter if they make gestures or imply you're slow—whatever. It's a performance; don't justify it. Embrace this discomfort and the power of knowing you can ask whatever you want and not be satisfied with just one answer.

MISSION 15: Today, you're going to take a different route to your usual destination (work, home, etc.). Explore a new path, even if it takes longer. Allow yourself the adventure of getting a little lost. If someone questions your route, simply say "I wanted a change of scenery."

MISSION 16: Today, you're going to cancel a last-minute commitment. It doesn't matter if it's a date, a meeting, or an outing with friends. Simply inform them you can't attend, without giving elaborate excuses. If they pressure you, repeat "something came up" and end the conversation without further explanation.

MISSION 17: This mission will be completed when you openly interrupt with an "I'm not interested" to someone discussing a topic that bores you, is irrelevant, or is simply shared criticism or toxicity. If you receive unsolicited service calls or sales pitches, this is a perfect opportunity. Don't feign interest out of courtesy, don't provide emotional support. If they pressure you, simply repeat "I'm really not interested" and change the subject.

MISSION 18: Today, you're going to buy an item from a store (something inexpensive, paid in cash) and return it after 10 minutes. Do this just for the feeling that, with the receipt and the unopened, unused item, you have the right to return it. If they ask "Why are you returning it?" Simply because you changed your mind. Be aware of the store's return policy before carrying out this mission; it's not about imposing a right, but about not feeling shame for exercising it.

MISSION 19: This mission will be completed when you respond to a compliment with simply "I know" instead of your usual modest response. Don't minimize your achievements or qualities. Accept the recognition without feeling obligated to return the compliment or downplay your success.

Example: "Hey, you look elegant!" "I know."

Or "This turned out really well!" "I know."

Appendix 3: The 10 Commandments of Truly Authentic People

Throughout this book, we've explored the art of stopping being excessively nice and starting to prioritize our own needs. We've talked about setting boundaries, saying "NO" without guilt, letting go of responsibility for others' emotions, and embracing our authenticity. But how do we refer to those who master this art? How do we describe these brave individuals who dare to live life on their own terms, without succumbing to the yoke of pleasing everyone?

The answer is simple: these people are truly authentic. They are individuals who have decided to be true to themselves above all else. This isn't about selfishness or lack of consideration for others, but rather about a deep respect for their own truth and well-being.

These authentic people understand they can't be everything to everyone. They know that constantly trying to please others is a recipe for exhaustion and resentment. Instead, they've learned to listen to their inner voice and honor their own needs and desires.

But take note: being authentic doesn't mean being insensitive or disrespectful. Truly authentic people don't trample others to maintain their authenticity. On the contrary, they understand that self-respect and respect for others go hand in hand. They know they can be true to themselves without belittling or hurting those around them.

Here, I want to present what I've chosen to call "The 10 Commandments of Truly Authentic People." These are ten ways of being that assertively complement the path we've been exploring throughout these pages.

Truly authentic people...

1. Listen more than they speak. Authentic people know that wisdom isn't found in constant talking, but in attentive listening. They don't need to fill every silence with empty words. Their presence speaks for itself.

2. Embrace their ignorance. No matter how brilliant they may be, authentic people understand there's always more to learn. They don't pretend to have all the answers but instead delight in the constant pursuit of knowledge.

3. Don't boast. Authentic people don't need to show off their achievements or abilities. They let their work and integrity speak for themselves, without fanfare or flourish. Their confidence comes from within, not from external validation.

4. Cultivate humility. Though they may be intelligent and capable, authentic people don't consider themselves superior to anyone. They understand that each person has their own value and that arrogance only blinds and isolates.

5. Prioritize quality over quantity in friendships. Authentic people may have a smaller circle of close friends because they don't settle for superficial relationships. They seek genuine connections with those around whom they can be themselves without filters.

6. Question boldly. Authentic people aren't afraid to ask probing questions that others might avoid. Their curiosity is insatiable, and they aren't content with half-answers. They dig deep until they get to the heart of matters.

7. Face problems head-on. Authentic people don't run from challenges. They know that the sooner a difficult situation is confronted, the better. They don't criticize for criticism's sake but seek solutions and opportunities for growth.

8. Devour knowledge from diverse sources. For authentic people, learning extends beyond books. They're open to learning from experiences, conversations, and reflective observation. Their minds are always hungry for new ideas.

9. Make no assumptions. While authentic people have honed their perception to extraordinary levels, they strive to understand and grasp others' true intentions and desires clearly. They don't take anything personally, nor do they make assumptions without reason.

10. Avoid unnecessary conflicts. Though firm in their convictions, authentic people don't seek pointless fights. They know how to choose their battles and don't waste energy on sterile arguments. Their security allows them to walk away from toxicity.

This is the ultimate goal behind this invitation to STOP BEING SO NICE: being authentic. The authenticity we've discussed isn't an excuse to do whatever we please without considering the consequences. It's a way of life based on honesty, integrity, and personal responsibility, where actions speak louder than any insipid niceness.

Appendix 4: Mephistophelian Contract

The contract on the following page is a sarcastic tool for setting boundaries with those who ask for favors without offering anything in return. With convoluted clauses, fine print, and cryptic text, this document transforms any favor into a bureaucratic trap of endless obligations.

The next time someone tries to take advantage of your good nature, simply present this contract and suggest, with a smile, that they sign it if they truly want your help. Their confusion will quickly turn to horror as they explore its labyrinthine clauses—if they manage to read them at all. This touch of dark humor won't just put moochers in their place; it will give you an untouchable reputation when it comes to future requests.

CONTRACT: INESCAPABLE AND INCOMPREHENSIBLE AGREEMENT FOR PERPETUAL AND NON-NEGOTIABLE PROVISION OF LIFELONG SERVICES

I, _____ (hereinafter referred to as "THE UNFORTUNATE," "THE ILL-FATED," "THE UNWARY," or "THE SUBJECT OF METAPHYSICAL MALFEASANCE"), being of sound mind (or in complete absence thereof), do hereby eternally bind myself under the following clause of everlasting renunciation of all moral, emotional, intellectual, psychological, or ontological recourse that might assist me, declaring myself in voluntary and unrestricted servitude to the omnipotent will of THE SUPREME ONE, without hope of redemption and with no horizon save an eternity of unconditional service in the abysses of space and time. **FIRST CLAUSE: UNKNOWABLE OBJECT OF THE CONTRACT:** THE UNFORTUNATE hereby condemns themselves to perform a myriad of services ad infinitum and ad nauseam, without respite or repose, directed toward satisfying the inscrutable whims and caprices of THE SUPREME ONE, who shall formulate such through the subtle vibration of their ineffable being, thus establishing an infinite concatenation of obligations that transcend the limits of human comprehension and extend beyond the confines of known reality. **SECOND CLAUSE: UNFATHOMABLE SCOPE AND PERPETUAL OBLIGATIONS.** The obligations, extending to the most remote corners of the multiverse, shall comprise Immediate and Uninterrupted Attention through the maintenance of perpetual vigilance to respond instantaneously to any requirement of THE SUPREME ONE, without expecting explanations or coherence of any kind, as well as the provision of Useless and Absurd Services including, without limitation, the counting and classification of each grain of sand in unexplored deserts, the meticulous documentation of phantasmagorical movements of one's own shadow, and the measurement with infinitesimal precision of wind characteristics in dimensions devoid of atmosphere, in addition to the Custodianship of Intangible Treasures through uninterrupted surveillance of relics and talismans lacking defined form or verifiable existence in any plane of consensual reality. **THIRD CLAUSE: SUPERHUMAN DEMANDS AND METAPHYSICAL ALTERATIONS.** THE UNFORTUNATE must maintain an unshakeable temperament and develop impossible abilities that defy the fundamental laws of physics and biology, including the capacity to sleep with eyes open while dreaming with them closed, the faculty to subsist exclusively on dew and starlight, and the gift of fractal ubiquity to serve simultaneously across multiple dimensions, all while maintaining a precarious balance between the most penetrating lucidity and the most unfathomable delirium. **FOURTH CLAUSE: INESCAPABLE WAIVERS AND COSMIC ABANDONMENT.** THE UNFORTUNATE irrevocably and absolutely waives all rights, privileges, or hope of redemption under any human, divine, or supernatural law, accepting their total abandonment to the caprices of THE SUPREME ONE, and acknowledging the futility of any attempt at appeal, resistance, or pursuit of clemency before celestial powers or infernal forces. **FIFTH CLAUSE: INFINITE PUNISHMENTS AND TORMENTS.** Non-compliance, delay, or mere hesitation in the execution of supreme mandates shall be punished through confinement in Borgesian labyrinths of impossible geometry, the torture of amplified mental echo that shall transform each thought into an unbearable cacophony, and the torment of eternal thirst before illusory oases that vanish to the rhythm of THE SUPREME ONE's mocking laughter. **FINAL CLAUSE: ACCEPTANCE OF ETERNAL CONDEMNATION.** By signing with blood, tears, and the indelible ink of their own misfortune, THE UNFORTUNATE accepts their existential nullity and eternal submission to the inscrutable designs of THE SUPREME ONE, renouncing all hope of salvation in the dungeons of cosmic absurdity, where each instant of their accursed existence shall be consecrated to the fulfillment of incomprehensible wills and indecipherable whims.

Signature

_____

About the Author

In addition to being a writer and speaker, Juan David Arbeláez is a Mentalist. A master of the power of the mind, he uses techniques in suggestion, body language, neurolinguistic programming, emotional intelligence, stage magic, and even probability to create the illusion of a sixth sense through his five senses.

His conferences, workshops, and show-talks have been presented to thousands of spectators and major Colombian companies including Bancolombia, EPM, UNE, Grupo Corona, Grupo Argos, Éxito, Grupo SURA, NUTRESA, and Grupo Familia, among others.

Juan David is also a Latin American champion of mentalism and is frequently invited to demonstrate his abilities and share his experiences on various television programs, including appearances on shows like DON FRANCISCO PRESENTA, where he has performed multiple times for the entire Latin American television audience.

His Facebook page has thousands of followers who regularly share and discuss his articles and videos with him.

★★★

Printed in Great Britain
by Amazon